AI Trends in 2025

Preface

Artificial intelligence (AI) is no longer a futuristic concept—it is a transformative force reshaping industries, economies, and societies. From autonomous systems that navigate our roads to intelligent algorithms that diagnose diseases, AI is unlocking possibilities that were once the realm of science fiction. Yet, as we stand on the brink of this technological revolution, it is essential to understand not only the potential of AI but also the challenges and responsibilities that come with it.

This book is a comprehensive exploration of the most significant trends and advancements in AI, from the rise of autonomous agents and the convergence of AI with quantum computing to the ethical imperatives of explainable AI and the privacy-preserving power of federated learning. Each chapter delves into a critical aspect of AI, offering insights into its evolution, applications, challenges, and future directions. Whether you are a researcher, practitioner, policymaker, or simply an AI enthusiast, this book aims to provide a clear and accessible guide to the technologies that are shaping our world.

The journey of writing this book has been both inspiring and humbling. It has reminded us of the incredible ingenuity of the human mind and the boundless potential of AI to solve some of the world's most pressing problems. At the same time, it has underscored the importance of approaching AI with care, ensuring that it is developed and deployed in ways that are ethical, transparent, and aligned with human values.

We hope this book serves as a valuable resource for anyone seeking to understand the present and future of AI. More importantly, we hope it sparks meaningful conversations about how we can harness the power of AI to create a better, more equitable world for all.

Acknowledgments

This book would not have been possible without the contributions of countless researchers, innovators, and thought leaders whose work has paved the way for the advancements we discuss. We are deeply grateful to the authors and organizations whose insights and discoveries have informed this book. A full list of references and acknowledgments can be found at the end of this book.

To the Reader

As you embark on this journey through the world of AI, we invite you to approach it with curiosity and an open mind. The future of AI is not predetermined—it is being shaped by the choices we make today. Together, we have the opportunity to ensure that AI serves as a force for good, empowering humanity to achieve its full potential.

Welcome to the future of AI. Let's explore it together.

Section 1: Foundations of AI

1. AI Agents: The Future of Autonomous Problem-Solving

What Are AI Agents?

AI agents represent a significant leap in artificial intelligence technology, moving beyond traditional AI models that primarily analyze data or provide recommendations. These autonomous systems are designed to understand, reason, plan, and execute tasks in a manner that solves complex problems without requiring constant human oversight. Unlike conventional AI, which often relies on predefined rules or human input to function, AI agents are capable of decomposing large, intricate issues into smaller, manageable tasks and taking actionable steps to resolve them. This ability to act autonomously makes AI agents a transformative force across various industries.

At their core, AI agents are systems that interact with their environment through inputs such as images, text, sounds, or sensor data. Once they process and interpret this information, they plan and execute actions to achieve specific goals. For example, an AI agent might control a thermostat to optimize energy usage or manage a global supply chain to ensure efficiency. These agents are not designed to mimic human thinking directly but instead operate by optimizing solutions through automation and machine learning.

This allows them to handle tasks that would be impractical or impossible for humans to manage efficiently.

The concept of AI agents is not entirely new, but the technology has evolved rapidly in recent years. Early AI systems were highly dependent on human input and control, limiting their effectiveness and scalability. However, advancements in machine learning, reinforcement learning, and multi-modal integration have enabled AI agents to become more autonomous and adaptable. By 2025, AI agents are expected to reach a tipping point, where they can handle complex, real-time tasks with a level of intelligence and autonomy that was once unimaginable.

The Evolution of AI Agents

The evolution of AI agents can be traced back to the early days of artificial intelligence, when systems were primarily rule-based and required significant human intervention. These early systems were limited in their ability to adapt to new situations or learn from experience. However, the advent of machine learning and deep learning has revolutionized the field, enabling AI agents to learn from data and improve their performance over time.

One of the key milestones in the evolution of AI agents was the development of reinforcement learning, a type of machine learning where agents learn by interacting with their environment and receiving feedback in the form of rewards or penalties. This approach has enabled AI agents to develop strategies for solving complex problems, such as playing games or controlling robots, without explicit instructions. Reinforcement learning has also paved the way for multi-agent systems, where multiple AI agents collaborate to achieve a common goal.

Another significant development has been the integration of multi-modal data, which allows AI agents to process and interpret information from various sources, such as text, images, and sensor data. This capability has made AI agents more versatile and capable of handling a wide range of tasks. For example, an AI agent in healthcare might analyze medical images, patient records, and sensor data from wearable devices to diagnose conditions and recommend treatments.

By 2025, AI agents are expected to become even more autonomous and adaptable, thanks to advances in distributed systems and self-learning algorithms. These systems will be able to work across multiple domains simultaneously, from healthcare and finance to logistics and customer service, without requiring major architectural changes. This flexibility will enable AI agents to tackle increasingly complex and dynamic environments, making them indispensable tools for solving real-world problems.

Main Applications of AI Agents

The versatility of AI agents makes them applicable across a wide range of industries, where they can automate complex decision-making and execution processes. Below are some of the key sectors where AI agents are expected to have a significant impact:

1. Healthcare: In the healthcare industry, AI agents have the potential to revolutionize patient care by autonomously monitoring patient data, predicting potential health issues, and adjusting treatment plans. For example, an AI agent could analyze data from wearable devices to detect early signs of a heart condition and recommend preventive measures. In hospitals, AI agents could assist doctors by analyzing medical images, identifying anomalies, and suggesting treatment options. This would not only improve patient outcomes but also reduce

the workload on healthcare professionals.

2. Finance: The finance industry is another area where AI agents are expected to play a crucial role. These agents can assist in trading by analyzing market data and executing trades in real time. They can also manage investment portfolios, providing personalized advice based on an individual's financial goals and risk tolerance. Additionally, AI agents can help detect fraudulent activities by analyzing transaction patterns and identifying suspicious behavior. By automating these tasks, AI agents can enhance efficiency and reduce the risk of human error.

3. Customer Service: AI agents are already making waves in the customer service industry, where they can handle everything from routine queries to complex troubleshooting. For example, an AI agent could assist customers with booking flights, resolving technical issues, or providing product recommendations. These agents can offer a personalized experience by analyzing customer data and tailoring their responses accordingly. As AI agents become more advanced, they will be able to handle increasingly complex interactions, reducing the need for human intervention.

4. Logistics and Supply Chain Management: In the logistics industry, AI agents can optimize routes, manage inventories, and predict demand fluctuations in real time. For example, an AI agent could analyze data from GPS systems, weather forecasts, and traffic patterns to determine the most efficient delivery routes. In supply chain management, AI agents can monitor inventory levels, predict shortages, and automatically reorder supplies when necessary. This would help companies reduce costs, improve efficiency, and ensure timely delivery of goods.

5. Sports and Entertainment: AI agents are also finding applications in the

sports and entertainment industry, where they can analyze game data and provide insights into strategy and player performance. For example, an AI agent could analyze video footage of a soccer match to identify patterns in player movements and suggest strategies for improving performance. In the entertainment industry, AI agents can help create personalized content recommendations based on a user's viewing history and preferences.

6. Manufacturing: In the manufacturing sector, AI agents can optimize production processes by monitoring equipment performance, predicting maintenance needs, and identifying inefficiencies. For example, an AI

agent could analyze data from sensors on a production line to detect anomalies and suggest corrective actions. This would help manufacturers reduce downtime, improve product quality, and increase overall efficiency.

7. Energy and Utilities: AI agents can play a crucial role in the energy and utilities sector by optimizing energy consumption, predicting equipment failures, and managing renewable energy sources. For example, an AI agent could analyze data from smart meters to identify patterns in energy usage and suggest ways to reduce consumption. In the case of renewable energy, AI agents can predict fluctuations in energy

production from sources like solar and wind, ensuring a stable supply of electricity.

8. Transportation: The transportation industry is another area where AI agents are expected to have a significant impact. These agents can optimize traffic flow, manage autonomous vehicles, and predict maintenance needs for transportation infrastructure. For example, an AI agent could analyze data from traffic sensors to identify congestion hotspots and suggest alternative routes. In the case of autonomous vehicles, AI agents can navigate complex environments, avoid obstacles, and ensure passenger safety.

Challenges Ahead

While the potential of AI agents is immense, there are several challenges that need to be addressed to ensure their successful implementation. These challenges span ethical, technical, and operational domains, and addressing them will be crucial for the widespread adoption of AI agents.

1. Ethical Decision-Making: One of the most significant challenges associated with AI agents is ensuring that they make ethical decisions. As these agents become more autonomous, there is a risk that they may make decisions that have unintended consequences. For example, an AI agent in healthcare might recommend a treatment that

is not in the best interest of the patient, or an AI agent in finance might execute a trade that results in significant financial losses. Ensuring that AI agents adhere to ethical guidelines and make decisions that align with human values will be crucial.

2. Transparency and Explainability: Another challenge is ensuring that the decision-making process of AI agents is transparent and explainable. In many cases, AI agents operate as "black boxes," where the reasoning behind their decisions is not easily understood. This lack of transparency can be problematic, especially in sectors like healthcare and finance, where decisions can

have significant consequences. Developing methods to make AI agents more explainable will be essential for building trust and ensuring accountability.

3. Security and Privacy: The security of AI agents is another major concern. These agents rely on vast amounts of data, which may include sensitive information such as personal health records or financial data. Ensuring that this data is secure from external threats and that AI agents cannot be manipulated is paramount. Additionally, privacy issues arise when AI agents collect and analyze personal data. Striking a balance between leveraging data for AI agent functionality and protecting

individual privacy will be a key challenge.

4. Bias and Fairness: AI agents are only as good as the data they are trained on, and if this data contains biases, the agents may make unfair or discriminatory decisions. For example, an AI agent used in hiring processes might favor certain demographics over others if the training data is biased. Addressing these biases and ensuring that AI agents make fair and unbiased decisions will require continuous oversight and improvement.

5. Regulation and Governance: As AI agents become more prevalent, there will be a need for clear regulations and governance

frameworks to ensure their responsible use. This includes defining the roles and responsibilities of AI agents, establishing standards for their development and deployment, and creating mechanisms for accountability. Governments and organizations will need to work together to develop these frameworks and ensure that AI agents are used in a way that benefits society as a whole.

6. Integration with Existing Systems: Integrating AI agents with existing systems and processes can be challenging, especially in industries with legacy systems. Ensuring that AI agents can seamlessly interact

with these systems and that they do not disrupt existing workflows will be crucial for their successful implementation.

7. Scalability: As AI agents are deployed across various industries, ensuring that they can scale to handle large volumes of data and complex tasks will be essential. This will require advancements in distributed systems and cloud computing, as well as the development of more efficient algorithms.

8. Human-AI Collaboration: While AI agents are designed to operate autonomously, there will still be a need for human oversight and collaboration. Ensuring that humans and AI agents can work together

effectively will be crucial for maximizing the benefits of this technology. This includes developing interfaces that allow humans to interact with AI agents easily and providing training for workers to understand and work alongside these systems.

The Future of AI Agents

The future of AI agents is incredibly promising, with the potential to transform industries and solve some of the world's most complex problems. As these agents become more autonomous and adaptable, they will be able to handle tasks that were once thought to be the exclusive domain of humans. This will lead to increased efficiency, improved decision-making, and new opportunities for innovation.

One of the most exciting prospects for AI agents is their ability to collaborate across domains. For example, an AI agent in healthcare could share insights with an AI agent in finance to develop personalized health insurance plans. Similarly, an AI agent in logistics could collaborate with an AI agent in manufacturing to optimize supply chains. This cross-domain collaboration will enable AI agents to tackle complex, multi-faceted problems that require a holistic approach.

Another key trend in the future of AI agents is the development of self-learning systems. These systems will be able to learn from their experiences and improve their performance over time, without requiring explicit programming. This will enable AI agents to adapt to new challenges and environments, making them even more versatile and powerful.

As AI agents become more prevalent, there will also be a growing need for interdisciplinary collaboration. Experts in fields such as computer science, ethics, law, and sociology will need to work together to address the challenges associated with AI agents and ensure that they are used in a way that benefits society. This will require a holistic approach that considers not only the technical aspects of AI agents but also their social and ethical implications.

In conclusion, AI agents represent a significant advancement in artificial intelligence, with the potential to revolutionize industries and solve complex problems. While there are challenges that need to be addressed, the benefits of AI agents far outweigh the risks. As we move towards a future where AI agents are an integral part of our lives, it is essential to ensure that they are developed and deployed responsibly, with a focus on ethical decision-making, transparency, and collaboration. By doing so, we can harness the full potential of AI agents and create a better future for all.

2. Inference Computation: The Backbone of AI Decision-Making

What is Inference Computation?

Inference computation is a fundamental process in artificial intelligence (AI) that enables trained models to apply their learned knowledge to new, real-time data. After an AI system has been trained on large datasets, inference is the phase where the model "uses" its acquired knowledge to solve new, unseen problems. For example, an AI model trained to recognize objects in images will apply its learned patterns to classify objects in a new image. This step is crucial for AI's ability to make predictions, decisions, and provide actionable insights in real-world scenarios.

In traditional AI models, inference is typically fast and efficient, providing quick responses to inputs. This speed is ideal for tasks that require immediate results, such as image recognition, voice assistants, or answering user queries. However, as AI models grow in complexity, the nature of inference is evolving. In the future, AI systems will spend more time processing information, reasoning through different possibilities, and providing more thoughtful, accurate responses. This shift towards deeper, more nuanced inference will mark a significant improvement in AI's decision-making ability, enabling it to tackle increasingly complex problems.

The Evolution of Inference Computation

The evolution of inference computation has been driven by advancements in AI architecture, computational power, and the increasing complexity of real-world problems. Early AI systems were designed to perform relatively simple tasks, such as recognizing patterns in data or making basic predictions. These systems relied on straightforward algorithms and required minimal computational resources for inference. However, as AI applications expanded into more complex domains, such as healthcare, finance, and autonomous systems, the need for deeper and more sophisticated inference grew.

By 2025, inference computation is expected to undergo a significant transformation.

Current AI systems often prioritize speed, providing quick answers to questions or tasks. While this approach is effective for many applications, it can limit the depth of analysis and the quality of decision-making. With advancements in AI architecture and computational capabilities, models will spend more time analyzing data before making decisions. This deeper level of processing will lead to more accurate, context-aware outcomes, enabling AI to solve complex problems with a greater level of sophistication.

For example, in healthcare, AI will no longer just provide a quick diagnosis but will analyze a wide range of potential conditions, considering factors like medical history, genetic data, and current health trends to provide a more informed recommendation. In finance, AI will move beyond responding to market trends—it will analyze the broader economic context, integrate real-time data from various sources, and generate predictions that are more precise and actionable.

This shift will be powered by innovations in neural networks, attention mechanisms, and distributed learning, making it possible for AI to engage in deeper reasoning and more comprehensive decision-making. Additionally, by 2025, AI systems will be more flexible, able to work across diverse domains without needing extensive retraining, allowing developers to continually refine and optimize inference processes.

Main Applications of Next-Generation Inference Computation

The next-generation inference computation will have far-reaching impacts across several industries. Below are some of the key sectors where this technology is expected to make a significant difference:

1. Healthcare: In healthcare, AI systems will assist in diagnosing complex diseases and optimizing treatment plans based on a deeper understanding of patient data. For example, an AI model could analyze a patient's medical history, genetic information, and real-time health data to provide a personalized diagnosis and treatment plan. This level of analysis would enable

healthcare providers to make more informed decisions, improving patient outcomes and reducing the risk of misdiagnosis.

2. Finance: In the finance industry, AI models will provide more refined trading strategies and investment advice by analyzing broader, more intricate patterns in market behavior. For instance, an AI system could integrate data from global markets, economic indicators, and news sources to predict market trends and recommend investment opportunities. This would enable financial institutions to make more informed decisions, reducing risk and maximizing returns.

3. Customer Service: Customer service will benefit from AI's ability to provide highly accurate, personalized recommendations, improving satisfaction and efficiency. For example, an AI-powered chatbot could analyze a customer's purchase history, preferences, and previous interactions to provide tailored product recommendations or resolve issues more effectively. This would enhance the customer experience and reduce the workload on human agents.

4. Autonomous Vehicles: Autonomous vehicles will also see significant improvements, with AI making faster, more reliable decisions in

response to real-time data from sensors and cameras. For instance, an AI system in a self-driving car could analyze data from multiple sensors to detect obstacles, predict the behavior of other vehicles, and make split-second decisions to ensure passenger safety. This would enable autonomous vehicles to navigate complex environments more effectively, reducing the risk of accidents.

5. Manufacturing: In the manufacturing sector, AI systems will optimize production processes by analyzing data from sensors and machines in real time. For example, an AI model could monitor equipment performance, predict maintenance

needs, and identify inefficiencies in the production line. This would enable manufacturers to reduce downtime, improve product quality, and increase overall efficiency.

6. Energy and Utilities: AI systems will play a crucial role in the energy and utilities sector by optimizing energy consumption, predicting equipment failures, and managing renewable energy sources. For instance, an AI model could analyze data from smart meters to identify patterns in energy usage and suggest ways to reduce consumption. In the case of renewable energy, AI systems could predict fluctuations in energy production from sources like solar

and wind, ensuring a stable supply of electricity.

7. Retail: In the retail industry, AI systems will enhance the shopping experience by providing personalized recommendations and optimizing inventory management. For example, an AI model could analyze a customer's browsing history, purchase behavior, and preferences to suggest products they are likely to buy. Additionally, AI systems could monitor inventory levels, predict demand fluctuations, and automatically reorder products to ensure availability.

8. Transportation and Logistics: AI systems will optimize transportation and logistics by analyzing data from

GPS systems, traffic patterns, and weather forecasts. For instance, an AI model could determine the most efficient delivery routes, reducing fuel consumption and delivery times. In logistics, AI systems could monitor inventory levels, predict shortages, and automatically reorder supplies when necessary.

Challenges Ahead

Despite the significant benefits of next-generation inference computation, several challenges need to be addressed to ensure its successful implementation. These challenges span technical, ethical, and operational domains and require a holistic approach to overcome.

1. Balancing Speed and Depth: One of the biggest challenges is balancing the speed of inference with the depth of analysis. In many industries, decisions need to be made quickly, so making inference slower could introduce delays that are unacceptable. For example, in autonomous vehicles, split-second decisions are crucial for ensuring passenger safety. Developing AI systems that can reason deeply without slowing down response times will be a key area of focus.

2. Adaptability and Learning on the Fly: Another challenge is improving AI systems' ability to learn on the fly, without requiring complete retraining. This will be particularly

important as AI systems need to adapt to new data or unforeseen events without losing efficiency. For example, an AI model in finance should be able to adapt to sudden market changes without requiring extensive retraining. Developing methods for continuous learning and adaptation will be essential for ensuring the flexibility and scalability of AI systems.

3. Computational Cost and Resource Requirements: The computational cost of deeper inference will increase, requiring more energy and resources. This could lead to concerns about the environmental impact and scalability of AI systems. For instance, training and running

large AI models can consume significant amounts of energy, contributing to carbon emissions. Developing more energy-efficient algorithms and hardware will be crucial for reducing the environmental impact of AI systems.

4. Transparency and Accountability: As AI models become more sophisticated, ensuring they maintain transparency and accountability will be critical. The risk of AI becoming a "black box" will need to be addressed to ensure ethical use in areas like healthcare and finance. For example, if an AI system makes a decision that affects a patient's health or a financial investment, it should be possible to

understand the reasoning behind that decision. Developing methods for explainable AI (XAI) will be essential for building trust and ensuring accountability.

5. Data Privacy and Security: AI systems rely on vast amounts of data, which may include sensitive information such as personal health records or financial data. Ensuring that this data is secure from external threats and that AI agents cannot be manipulated is paramount. Additionally, privacy issues arise when AI systems collect and analyze personal data. Striking a balance between leveraging data for AI functionality and protecting

individual privacy will be a key challenge.

6. Bias and Fairness: AI systems are only as good as the data they are trained on, and if this data contains biases, the models may make unfair or discriminatory decisions. For example, an AI system used in hiring processes might favor certain demographics over others if the training data is biased. Addressing these biases and ensuring that AI systems make fair and unbiased decisions will require continuous oversight and improvement.

7. Regulation and Governance: As AI systems become more prevalent, there will be a need for clear regulations and governance

frameworks to ensure their responsible use. This includes defining the roles and responsibilities of AI systems, establishing standards for their development and deployment, and creating mechanisms for accountability. Governments and organizations will need to work together to develop these frameworks and ensure that AI systems are used in a way that benefits society as a whole.

8. Integration with Existing Systems: Combining AI systems with current infrastructure and workflows can be difficult, particularly in sectors reliant on outdated or legacy technologies. Ensuring that AI

systems can seamlessly interact with these systems and that they do not disrupt existing workflows will be crucial for their successful implementation.

The Future of Inference Computation

The future of inference computation is incredibly promising, with the potential to transform industries and solve some of the world's most complex problems. As AI systems become more autonomous and adaptable, they will be able to handle tasks that were once thought to be the exclusive domain of humans. This will lead to increased efficiency, improved decision-making, and new opportunities for innovation.

One of the most exciting prospects for inference computation is its ability to enable cross-domain collaboration. For example, an AI system in healthcare could share insights with an AI system in finance to develop personalized health insurance plans. Similarly, an AI system in logistics could collaborate with an AI system in manufacturing to optimize supply chains. This cross-domain collaboration will enable AI systems to tackle complex, multi-faceted problems that require a holistic approach.

Another key trend in the future of inference computation is the development of self-learning systems. These systems will be able to learn from their experiences and improve their performance over time, without requiring explicit programming.

This will enable AI systems to adapt to new challenges and environments, making them even more versatile and powerful.

As AI systems become more prevalent, there will also be a growing need for interdisciplinary collaboration. Experts in fields such as computer science, ethics, law, and sociology will need to work together to address the challenges associated with AI systems and ensure that they are used in a way that benefits society. Addressing this challenge demands a comprehensive strategy that takes into account not just the technical dimensions of AI systems, but also their broader societal and ethical consequences.

In conclusion, inference computation is a critical component of AI systems, enabling them to apply learned knowledge to new, real-time data. As AI systems evolve, the nature of inference computation is shifting towards deeper, more nuanced analysis, enabling more accurate and context-aware decision-making. While there are challenges that need to be addressed, the benefits of next-generation inference computation far outweigh the risks. By developing AI systems that are transparent, adaptable, and energy-efficient, we can harness the full potential of this technology and create a better future for all.

3. Very Large Models (VLMs) vs. Very Small Models (VSMs): The Future of AI Scaling

What Are Very Large Models (VLMs)?

Very Large Models (VLMs) represent the pinnacle of artificial intelligence (AI) scalability, built on networks of parameters that can number in the trillions. These models are designed to process and understand complex data at a scale that mimics human-like reasoning, enabling them to tackle a wide range of tasks across multiple domains. Examples of VLMs include GPT-4, which has demonstrated remarkable capabilities in text generation, language translation, image recognition, and even medical diagnosis. The sheer size of these models allows them to generalize across diverse problems, making them highly versatile and powerful.

The development of VLMs is driven by advancements in hardware, such as GPUs and TPUs, as well as innovations in training algorithms and data availability. These models require immense computational power and storage to train and deploy, but their size gives them unmatched capabilities in terms of generalization and problem-solving. For instance, a VLM trained on a diverse dataset can perform tasks ranging from generating human-like text to diagnosing diseases based on medical images.

By 2025, the scale of VLMs is expected to grow dramatically, with models potentially reaching up to 50 trillion parameters. This growth will be fueled by innovations in hardware, more efficient training algorithms, and the increasing demand for sophisticated AI applications. These models will be incredibly versatile, capable of applying their knowledge across diverse fields without needing extensive retraining. This makes them highly valuable for industries like healthcare, finance, and autonomous systems, where complex problem-solving is required.

However, VLMs come with significant challenges. Their massive computational and energy demands raise concerns about sustainability, as training and deploying these models can consume vast amounts of electricity and contribute to carbon emissions. Additionally, the opaque nature of VLMs—often referred to as "black box" behavior—can create problems in terms of accountability, ethics, and transparency. Understanding how these models arrive at their decisions is crucial for ensuring their responsible use, especially in high-stakes applications like healthcare and finance.

What Are Very Small Models (VSMs)?

In contrast to VLMs, Very Small Models (VSMs) are optimized to run on edge devices, such as smartphones, IoT devices, and other consumer-grade hardware. These models are small—often just a few billion parameters—but are highly efficient and tailored for specific tasks. VSMs excel in real-time decision-making applications that require low-latency processing, such as speech recognition, image classification, and language translation. Their compact size and efficiency make them ideal for deployment on devices with limited computational resources.

By 2025, VSMs will become even more powerful, thanks to advancements in model optimization techniques such as pruning, distillation, and quantization. Pruning involves removing unnecessary parameters from a model to reduce its size, while distillation transfers knowledge from a large model to a smaller one. Quantization reduces the precision of the model's parameters, making it more efficient without significantly compromising performance. These techniques will enable VSMs to deliver sophisticated performance in highly specialized tasks, allowing them to outperform larger models in specific, defined areas.

VSMs will be integrated into a wide range of consumer electronics and autonomous systems, enabling real-time AI processing directly on devices, with no need for cloud computing. For example, a smartphone equipped with a VSM could perform real-time language translation or image recognition without relying on external servers. Similarly, an autonomous vehicle could use a VSM to make split-second decisions based on data from its sensors and cameras. This capability will make VSMs indispensable for applications that require low-latency processing and high efficiency.

Evolution and Future Developments

The future of AI will be shaped by the evolution of both VLMs and VSMs, each serving distinct but complementary roles. VLMs will continue to grow in size and capability, driven by advancements in hardware and training algorithms. These models will revolutionize industries like healthcare and autonomous systems by providing human-like problem-solving capabilities across a range of tasks. For example, a VLM in healthcare could analyze vast amounts of patient data to diagnose diseases, recommend treatments, and predict outcomes with unprecedented accuracy.

On the other hand, VSMs will become more efficient, specialized, and embedded into everyday devices. These models will dominate in real-time applications requiring low-latency processing, such as autonomous vehicles, consumer electronics, and healthcare monitoring devices. For instance, a VSM in a wearable device could monitor a user's health in real time, detecting anomalies and providing immediate feedback. Similarly, a VSM in a smart home system could optimize energy usage based on real-time data from sensors.

The coexistence of VLMs and VSMs will enable a new era of AI applications, where large-scale problem-solving and real-time processing are seamlessly integrated. For example, a VLM in the cloud could analyze vast amounts of data to generate insights, while a VSM on a device could use those insights to make real-time decisions. This synergy will unlock new possibilities for AI, enabling it to tackle increasingly complex and dynamic challenges.

Main Applications

The applications of VLMs and VSMs span a wide range of industries, each leveraging the unique strengths of these models. Below are some of the key sectors where VLMs and VSMs are expected to make a significant impact:

1. Healthcare: VLMs will revolutionize healthcare by providing human-like problem-solving capabilities across a range of tasks. For example, a VLM could analyze medical images, patient records, and genetic data to diagnose diseases, recommend treatments, and predict outcomes. In contrast, VSMs will be used in healthcare monitoring devices, such as wearables, to provide real-time feedback on a user's health. For

instance, a VSM in a smartwatch could monitor heart rate, detect anomalies, and alert the user to potential health issues.

2. Finance: In the finance industry, VLMs will be used to analyze vast amounts of market data, predict trends, and generate investment strategies. For example, a VLM could integrate data from global markets, economic indicators, and news sources to provide insights into market behavior. VSMs, on the other hand, will be used in real-time trading applications, where low-latency processing is crucial. For instance, a VSM in a trading algorithm could analyze market data

in real time and execute trades with minimal delay.

3. Autonomous Systems: VLMs will play a crucial role in autonomous systems, such as self-driving cars and drones, by providing human-like problem-solving capabilities. For example, a VLM in a self-driving car could analyze data from sensors and cameras to navigate complex environments and make split-second decisions. VSMs will be used in real-time processing applications, such as obstacle detection and collision avoidance. For instance, a VSM in a drone could analyze data from its sensors to detect obstacles and adjust its flight path in real time.

4. Consumer Electronics: VSMs will dominate in consumer electronics, where real-time processing and efficiency are crucial. For example, a VSM in a smartphone could perform real-time language translation, image recognition, and speech recognition. Similarly, a VSM in a smart home system could optimize energy usage based on real-time data from sensors.

5. Creative Industries: VLMs will revolutionize the creative industries by providing human-like capabilities in tasks such as text generation, image creation, and music composition. For example, a VLM could generate a novel, create a piece of art, or compose a symphony

based on a set of inputs. VSMs, on the other hand, will be used in real-time creative applications, such as video editing and live performance. For instance, a VSM in a video editing software could analyze footage in real time and suggest edits based on the user's preferences.

6. Retail: In the retail industry, VLMs will be used to analyze customer data, predict trends, and optimize inventory management. For example, a VLM could analyze a customer's purchase history, preferences, and browsing behavior to provide personalized recommendations. VSMs will be used in real-time applications, such as checkout

systems and customer service. For instance, a VSM in a checkout system could analyze data from sensors to detect items and process payments in real time.

7. Energy and Utilities: In the energy and utilities industry, Vision-Language Models (VLMs) will be instrumental in processing large datasets to enhance energy efficiency and forecast potential equipment malfunctions. For example, a VLM could analyze data from smart meters to identify patterns in energy usage and suggest ways to reduce consumption. VSMs will be used in real-time applications, such as monitoring and control systems. For instance, a VSM

in a smart grid could analyze data from sensors to detect anomalies and adjust energy distribution in real time.

Challenges Ahead

Despite their immense potential, both VLMs and VSMs face significant challenges that need to be addressed to ensure their successful implementation. These challenges span technical, ethical, and operational domains and require a holistic approach to overcome.

1. Scalability and Efficiency: For VLMs, scaling up these models without compromising computational efficiency or energy consumption will be a key challenge. Training and deploying VLMs require vast

amounts of computational resources, which can be costly and environmentally unsustainable. Developing more efficient training algorithms and hardware will be crucial for reducing the environmental impact of VLMs.

2. Transparency and Accountability: The "black box" nature of VLMs raises serious ethical concerns, as it can be difficult to understand how these models arrive at their decisions. Ensuring transparency and accountability will be crucial for the responsible use of VLMs, especially in high-stakes applications like healthcare and finance. Developing methods for explainable

AI (XAI) will be essential for building trust and ensuring accountability.

3. Balancing Performance and Size: For VSMs, balancing performance and size remains a challenge. Ensuring that these smaller models can handle specialized tasks without overloading edge devices will require further advancements in hardware and optimization techniques. Developing more efficient algorithms and hardware will be crucial for ensuring the scalability and performance of VSMs.

4. Data Privacy and Security: Both VLMs and VSMs rely on vast amounts of data, which may include sensitive information such as personal health records or financial

data. Ensuring that this data is secure from external threats and that AI agents cannot be manipulated is paramount. Additionally, privacy issues arise when AI systems collect and analyze personal data. Striking a balance between leveraging data for AI functionality and protecting individual privacy will be a key challenge.

5. Bias and Fairness: AI systems are only as good as the data they are trained on, and if this data contains biases, the models may make unfair or discriminatory decisions. Addressing these biases and ensuring that AI systems make fair and unbiased decisions will require

continuous oversight and improvement.

6. Regulation and Governance: As AI systems become more prevalent, there will be a need for clear regulations and governance frameworks to ensure their responsible use. This includes defining the roles and responsibilities of AI systems, establishing standards for their development and deployment, and creating mechanisms for accountability. Governments and organizations will need to work together to develop these frameworks and ensure that AI systems are used in a way that benefits society as a whole.

7. Integration with Existing Systems: Combining AI systems with current infrastructure and workflows can be difficult, particularly in sectors reliant on outdated or legacy technologies. Ensuring that AI systems can seamlessly interact with these systems and that they do not disrupt existing workflows will be crucial for their successful implementation.

The Future of VLMs and VSMs

The future of AI will be shaped by the coexistence and collaboration of VLMs and VSMs, each serving distinct but complementary roles. VLMs will continue to grow in size and capability, driven by advancements in hardware and training algorithms. These models will revolutionize industries like healthcare and autonomous systems by providing human-like problem-solving capabilities across a range of tasks. On the other hand, VSMs will become more efficient, specialized, and embedded into everyday devices, enabling real-time AI processing in applications that require low-latency and high efficiency.

The synergy between VLMs and VSMs will unlock new possibilities for AI, enabling it to tackle increasingly complex and dynamic challenges. For example, a VLM in the cloud could analyze vast amounts of data to generate insights, while a VSM on a device could use those insights to make real-time decisions. This integration will enable AI to operate at both the macro and micro levels, providing solutions that are both comprehensive and immediate.

In conclusion, VLMs and VSMs represent two sides of the same coin, each offering unique strengths and capabilities. While VLMs excel in large-scale problem-solving and generalization, VSMs are optimized for real-time processing and efficiency. By addressing the challenges associated with these models and leveraging their complementary strengths, we can unlock the full potential of AI and create a better future for all.

4. Edge AI: Deploying AI Models on Edge Devices for Real-Time, Low-Latency Performance

Introduction

The rapid proliferation of Internet of Things (IoT) devices, coupled with advancements in artificial intelligence (AI), has given rise to a transformative paradigm known as Edge AI. Edge AI refers to the deployment of AI models directly on edge devices—such as smartphones, sensors, drones, and industrial machines—rather than relying on centralized cloud servers. By handling data on local devices, Edge AI allows for instant decision-making, lowers delays, improves privacy, and reduces the need for extensive bandwidth. This approach is particularly critical in applications where immediate responses are essential, such as autonomous vehicles, healthcare monitoring, and industrial automation.

As we move into 2025 and beyond, Edge AI is poised to become a cornerstone of the AI ecosystem, driving innovation across industries and enabling smarter, more responsive technologies. This section explores the principles of Edge AI, its evolution, key applications, challenges, and the future of this groundbreaking technology.

What is Edge AI?

Edge AI involves running AI algorithms and models directly on edge devices, which are typically located close to the data source.In contrast to conventional cloud-based AI, which relies on sending data to distant servers for analysis, Edge AI performs data processing directly on the device or through nearby edge servers. This decentralized approach offers several advantages, including faster response times, reduced reliance on internet connectivity, and enhanced data privacy.

Key Principles of Edge AI

1. Local Processing: Data is processed on the device or at the edge of the network, eliminating the need to transmit large volumes of data to centralized servers.

2. Real-Time Performance: Edge AI enables real-time decision-making, which is critical for applications like autonomous driving and industrial automation.

3. Privacy and Security: By keeping data on the device, Edge AI reduces the risk of data breaches and ensures compliance with privacy regulations.

4. Bandwidth Efficiency: Edge AI significantly decreases the necessity for data transmission, cutting down on bandwidth consumption and related expenses.

Why Edge AI Matters

- Low Latency: Edge AI removes the latency caused by transmitting data to and from the cloud, allowing for quicker and more immediate responses.

- Scalability: Edge AI allows for the deployment of AI models across millions of devices, making it highly scalable.

- Resilience: Edge AI systems can operate independently of cloud connectivity, ensuring functionality even in remote or unstable environments.

- Cost Efficiency: By reducing data transfer and storage costs, Edge AI offers a more economical solution for AI deployment.

The Evolution of Edge AI

The concept of Edge AI has evolved alongside advancements in hardware, software, and connectivity. Early AI systems relied heavily on centralized cloud infrastructure due to the computational demands of AI models. However, the rise of IoT devices, the need for real-time processing, and growing concerns about data privacy have driven the shift toward edge computing.

Key Milestones in Edge AI

- Early IoT Devices: The first generation of IoT devices focused on data collection and transmission, with limited processing capabilities.

- Advancements in Hardware: The development of powerful, energy-efficient processors (e.g., GPUs, TPUs, and specialized AI chips) enabled AI models to run on edge devices.

- 5G Connectivity: The rollout of 5G networks provided the high-speed, low-latency connectivity needed to support Edge AI applications.

- AI Model Optimization: Techniques like model quantization, pruning, and distillation made it possible to run complex AI models on resource-constrained devices.

The Future of Edge AI (2025 and Beyond)

By 2025, Edge AI will continue to evolve, driven by advancements in hardware, algorithms, and connectivity. Key trends include:

- AI at the Extreme Edge: Deploying AI models on ultra-low-power devices, such as sensors and wearables.

- Federated Learning Integration: Combining Edge AI with federated learning to enable collaborative model training across devices.

- Edge AI as a Service: Offering Edge AI platforms and tools as cloud-based services to democratize access.

- Autonomous Edge Systems: Developing self-learning edge

systems that can adapt to changing environments and user needs.

Applications of Edge AI

Edge AI has far-reaching applications across industries, enabling real-time, low-latency performance in a wide range of scenarios. Below are some of the key areas where Edge AI is making an impact:

1. Autonomous Vehicles

- Real-Time Decision-Making: Edge AI enables self-driving cars to process sensor data (e.g., cameras, LiDAR) in real time, allowing for immediate responses to road conditions.
- Safety and Reliability: By reducing reliance on cloud connectivity, Edge AI ensures that autonomous vehicles

can operate safely even in areas with poor internet access.

2. Healthcare

- Wearable Devices: Edge AI powers wearable devices that monitor vital signs (e.g., heart rate, blood pressure) and provide real-time feedback to users.

- Remote Diagnostics: Edge AI enables medical devices to analyze patient data locally, reducing the need for data transfers and ensuring timely diagnoses.

3. Industrial Automation

- Predictive Maintenance: Edge AI analyzes data from sensors on machinery to predict failures and schedule maintenance, reducing downtime and costs.

- Quality Control: Edge AI enables real-time inspection of products on production lines, ensuring quality and reducing waste.

4. Smart Cities

- Traffic Management: Edge AI processes data from traffic cameras and sensors to optimize traffic flow and reduce congestion.

- Public Safety: Edge AI enables real-time analysis of surveillance footage to detect and respond to security threats.

5. Retail

- Personalized Shopping: Edge AI powers smart shelves and kiosks that provide personalized recommendations to shoppers based on their behavior.

- Inventory Management: Edge AI analyzes data from in-store sensors to optimize inventory levels and reduce stockouts.

6. Agriculture

- Precision Farming: Edge AI processes data from drones and sensors to monitor crop health, optimize irrigation, and predict yields.
- Livestock Monitoring: Edge AI enables real-time tracking of livestock health and behavior, improving farm management.

7. Telecommunications

- Network Optimization: Edge AI analyzes data from network devices to optimize performance and reduce latency.
- Customer Experience: Edge AI enables real-time analysis of customer interactions to improve service quality.

Challenges in Edge AI

Despite its potential, Edge AI faces several significant challenges that must be addressed to ensure its successful implementation.

1. Hardware Limitations

- Edge devices often have limited computational power, memory, and energy resources, making it challenging to run complex AI models.

2. Model Optimization

- AI models must be optimized for edge deployment, often requiring trade-offs between accuracy, size, and speed.

3. Data Privacy

- While Edge AI reduces the risk of data breaches, it also requires robust security measures to protect data on the device.

4. Connectivity

- Edge AI systems must be able to operate in environments with limited or intermittent connectivity.

5. Scalability

- Deploying and managing AI models across millions of edge devices requires scalable infrastructure and tools.

6. Interoperability

- Ensuring that Edge AI systems can work seamlessly with existing IoT and cloud infrastructure is a complex task.

The Future of Edge AI

The future of Edge AI is bright, with numerous opportunities for innovation and impact. By 2025 and beyond, Edge AI will play a central role in shaping the development and deployment of AI technologies.

Key Trends

- AI at the Extreme Edge: Deploying AI models on ultra-low-power devices, such as sensors and wearables.

- Federated Learning Integration: Combining Edge AI with federated learning to enable collaborative model training across devices.

- Edge AI as a Service: Offering Edge AI platforms and tools as cloud-based services to democratize access.

- Autonomous Edge Systems: Developing self-learning edge systems that can adapt to changing environments and user needs.

Conclusion

Edge AI represents a paradigm shift in AI deployment, enabling real-time, low-latency performance across a wide range of applications. By 2025, Edge AI will revolutionize industries, drive innovation, and empower individuals and organizations to harness the power of AI at the edge. However, realizing this vision requires addressing significant technical, ethical, and regulatory challenges. Through collaboration, innovation, and a commitment to privacy and fairness, we can unlock the full potential of Edge AI and create a future where AI serves as a force for good, benefiting all of humanity.

5. Self-Supervised Learning and Self-Supervised Representation Learning: Unlocking the Power of Unlabeled Data

Introduction

The field of artificial intelligence (AI) has made remarkable strides in recent years, driven largely by advances in supervised learning, where models are trained on labeled datasets. However, the reliance on labeled data poses significant challenges, as acquiring high-quality annotations is often expensive, time-consuming, and impractical for many applications. Self-Supervised Learning (SSL) and Self-Supervised Representation Learning have emerged as transformative approaches to address these limitations. By enabling AI models to learn from vast amounts of unlabeled data, SSL uncovers patterns, structures, and insights without the need for explicit supervision. This paradigm shift is revolutionizing AI, making it more scalable, efficient, and applicable to a wider range of domains.

By 2025 and beyond, self-supervised learning is expected to play a pivotal role in advancing AI capabilities, particularly in areas where labeled data is scarce or difficult to obtain. This section explores the principles of SSL, its evolution, key applications, challenges, and the future of this groundbreaking technology.

What is Self-Supervised Learning?

Self-Supervised Learning is a machine learning paradigm where models learn to understand data by generating their own labels or supervisory signals from the input data itself. Unlike supervised learning, which relies on externally provided labels, SSL leverages the inherent structure and relationships within the data to create meaningful learning tasks. These tasks, often referred to as "pretext tasks," enable the model to learn rich representations of the data, which can then be fine-tuned for specific downstream tasks.

Key Principles of Self-Supervised Learning

1. Unlabeled Data Utilization: SSL leverages vast amounts of unlabeled data, which is often more abundant and easier to obtain than labeled data.

2. Pretext Tasks: Models are trained on tasks designed to exploit the structure of the data, such as predicting missing parts of an image or reconstructing a sentence.

3. Representation Learning: SSL focuses on learning high-quality, general-purpose representations of the data that can be transferred to various downstream tasks.

4. Transfer Learning: The representations learned through SSL can be fine-tuned on smaller labeled datasets for specific applications, such as image classification or natural language processing.

Why Self-Supervised Learning Matters

- Scalability: SSL enables the use of massive, unlabeled datasets, making it highly scalable.

- Cost Efficiency: By reducing the need for labeled data, SSL lowers the cost of training AI models.

- Generalization: SSL models learn more robust and generalizable representations, improving performance on downstream tasks.

- Domain Adaptability: SSL is particularly useful in domains where labeled data is scarce, such as healthcare and scientific research.

The Evolution of Self-Supervised Learning

The concept of self-supervised learning has its roots in early attempts to leverage unlabeled data for machine learning. However, it has gained significant traction in recent years due to advancements in deep learning, computational power, and the availability of large-scale datasets.

Key Milestones in Self-Supervised Learning

- Early Approaches: Early SSL methods focused on simple pretext tasks, such as predicting the next word in a sentence or filling in missing pixels in an image.

- Deep Learning Revolution: The advent of deep learning enabled more sophisticated SSL techniques, such as autoencoders and generative adversarial networks (GANs).

- Contrastive Learning: Contrastive learning, a popular SSL approach, involves learning representations by contrasting positive and negative samples. Techniques like SimCLR and MoCo have achieved state-of-the-art performance in image and text representation learning.

- Transformer Models: The rise of transformer-based models, such as BERT and GPT, has demonstrated the power of SSL in natural language processing (NLP). These models are pre-trained on large text corpora using SSL objectives and fine-tuned for specific tasks.

The Future of Self-Supervised Learning (2025 and Beyond)

By 2025, SSL will continue to evolve, driven by advancements in algorithms, hardware, and data availability. Key trends include:

- Multimodal SSL: Extending SSL to handle multiple data modalities, such as text, images, and audio, to learn richer representations.

- Cross-Domain SSL: Developing SSL techniques that can transfer knowledge across different domains and tasks.

- Self-Supervised Reinforcement Learning: Combining SSL with reinforcement learning to enable agents to learn from unlabeled environments.

- Scalable SSL Frameworks: Creating scalable and efficient SSL frameworks that can handle massive datasets and complex models.

Applications of Self-Supervised Learning

Self-Supervised Learning has far-reaching applications across industries, enabling the development of powerful AI models that can learn from unlabeled data. Below are some of the key areas where SSL is making an impact:

1. Natural Language Processing (NLP)

- Language Models: SSL has revolutionized NLP by enabling the development of large-scale language models like BERT, GPT, and T5. These models are pre-trained on vast text corpora using SSL objectives and fine-tuned for tasks such as text classification, translation, and summarization.
- Chatbots and Virtual Assistants: SSL-powered language models

enable more natural and context-aware interactions with chatbots and virtual assistants.

2. Computer Vision

- Image Recognition: SSL techniques like contrastive learning have achieved state-of-the-art performance in image classification, object detection, and segmentation.

- Medical Imaging: SSL enables the analysis of medical images (e.g., X-rays, MRIs) without the need for extensive labeled datasets, improving diagnostic accuracy and efficiency.

- Autonomous Vehicles: SSL helps autonomous vehicles understand and interpret visual data from cameras and sensors, enhancing safety and reliability.

3. Healthcare

- Drug Discovery: SSL can analyze molecular structures and biological data to identify potential drug candidates, accelerating the drug discovery process.
- Patient Monitoring: SSL enables the analysis of unlabeled patient data, such as electronic health records (EHRs), to predict health outcomes and recommend treatments.

4. Robotics

- Unsupervised Skill Acquisition: SSL allows robots to learn skills and behaviors from unlabeled data, such as video demonstrations or sensor readings.

- Environment Understanding: SSL helps robots understand and navigate complex environments by learning representations of sensory data.

5. Finance

- Fraud Detection: SSL can analyze transaction data to detect fraudulent activity without the need for labeled examples.

- Market Analysis: SSL enables the analysis of unlabeled financial data, such as stock prices and news articles, to predict market trends and inform investment strategies.

6. Scientific Research

- Genomics: SSL can analyze genomic data to identify patterns and relationships, advancing research in genetics and personalized medicine.
- Climate Modeling: SSL enables the analysis of climate data to predict weather patterns and inform climate change mitigation strategies.

Challenges in Self-Supervised Learning

Despite its potential, Self-Supervised Learning faces several significant challenges that must be addressed to ensure its successful implementation.

1. Pretext Task Design

- Designing effective pretext tasks that capture the underlying structure of the data is a complex and domain-specific challenge.

2. Evaluation Metrics

- Evaluating the quality of learned representations in SSL is difficult, as there is no direct measure of performance on the pretext tasks.

3. Data Quality

- SSL relies on the availability of large, diverse, and high-quality unlabeled datasets, which may not always be available.

4. Computational Resources

- Training SSL models on large datasets requires significant computational resources, which can be a barrier for smaller organizations.

5. Transferability

- Ensuring that the representations learned through SSL are transferable to a wide range of downstream tasks is a key challenge.

6. Ethical Considerations

- SSL models trained on large datasets may inadvertently learn and perpetuate biases present in the data, raising ethical concerns.

The Future of Self-Supervised Learning

The future of Self-Supervised Learning is bright, with numerous opportunities for innovation and impact. By 2025 and beyond, SSL will play a central role in advancing AI capabilities and enabling new applications.

Key Trends

- Multimodal SSL: Extending SSL to handle multiple data modalities, such as text, images, and audio, to learn richer representations.

- Cross-Domain SSL: Developing SSL techniques that can transfer knowledge across different domains and tasks.

- Self-Supervised Reinforcement Learning: Combining SSL with reinforcement learning to enable agents to learn from unlabeled environments.

- Scalable SSL Frameworks: Creating scalable and efficient SSL frameworks that can handle massive datasets and complex models.

Conclusion

Self-supervised learning represents a paradigm shift in AI, enabling models to learn from vast amounts of unlabeled data and uncover patterns and insights that were previously inaccessible. By 2025, SSL will revolutionize industries, drive innovation, and empower individuals and organizations to harness the power of AI in new and exciting ways. However, realizing this vision requires addressing significant technical, ethical, and regulatory challenges. Through collaboration, innovation, and a commitment to fairness and transparency, we can unlock the full potential of Self-Supervised Learning and create a future where AI serves as a force for good, benefiting all of humanity.

Section 2: Emerging AI Technologies

1. Frontier AI Use Cases: The Next Wave of Transformation

What Are Frontier AI Use Cases?

Frontier AI use cases represent the cutting-edge applications where artificial intelligence (AI) is not merely a tool but a transformative force, capable of solving complex problems and driving significant changes across industries. These use cases go beyond traditional AI applications, which often focus on automating repetitive tasks or providing recommendations. Instead, frontier AI use cases involve systems that operate with a level of sophistication and autonomy that was previously unimaginable. These systems are designed to take on dynamic, proactive roles, enabling them to handle complex, multi-step tasks and make decisions with minimal human intervention.

The evolution of AI is enabling systems to move from basic automation to more advanced, autonomous functionalities. For example, customer service AI systems are no longer just programmed to answer basic questions—they are evolving into intelligent agents capable of diagnosing problems, providing solutions, and even handling intricate issues on their own. These systems are becoming increasingly adept at simulating human-like interactions, moving from basic responses to meaningful, nuanced conversations that enhance the user experience.

In the field of information technology (IT), frontier AI use cases are ushering in a new era where systems self-manage. Instead of relying on human administrators to troubleshoot and optimize networks, AI will anticipate issues before they arise and make real-time adjustments, ensuring that systems run efficiently without human intervention. This shift from reactive to proactive management is transforming the way IT systems operate, reducing downtime and improving overall performance.

Security is another domain where frontier AI is making significant strides. As AI matures, it will play a key role in identifying security vulnerabilities and responding to potential breaches autonomously. This capability drastically reduces the need for manual intervention in real-time threat detection and mitigation, making cybersecurity more efficient and effective. AI-driven security systems can analyze vast amounts of data to detect anomalies, predict potential threats, and take immediate action to neutralize them.

The power of frontier AI use cases lies in the ability to process and analyze vast amounts of data in a way that leads to smarter, more informed decisions. AI systems that once worked within a limited context are evolving to manage millions of data points, offering deep, real-time insights that will transform business operations, customer relations, and cybersecurity. These systems are not just tools for automation; they are becoming active agents that drive innovation and operational efficiency across industries.

The Evolution of Frontier AI Use Cases in 2025

By 2025, AI will be deeply integrated into nearly every industry, with its role evolving from a reactive tool to an active agent driving innovation and operational efficiency. This evolution will be driven by advancements in AI architecture, computational power, and data availability, enabling AI systems to handle increasingly complex tasks with greater autonomy and sophistication.

In customer service, AI will not only answer questions but predict customer needs based on historical data, behavioral patterns, and emerging trends. These systems will be able to anticipate problems and offer proactive solutions, enhancing customer satisfaction and reducing the need for human intervention. For example, an AI-driven customer service system could analyze a customer's purchase history and browsing behavior to predict their needs and offer personalized recommendations before the customer even makes a request. This level of proactive service will transform the customer experience, making it more seamless and satisfying.

In IT, the AI-driven future will see self-healing systems that identify and resolve network issues before they become disruptive. These autonomous networks will ensure high performance and minimal downtime, while also adapting to shifts in usage patterns in real time. For instance, an AI system could monitor network traffic and predict potential bottlenecks, making adjustments to optimize performance before any issues arise. This capability will be particularly valuable in industries that rely on high-performance IT infrastructure, such as finance, healthcare, and e-commerce.

Security AI will advance beyond simple detection, evolving into systems that can neutralize threats autonomously by identifying novel attack vectors and mitigating them without human oversight. Cybersecurity operations will increasingly be driven by AI systems capable of learning and adapting to new types of threats. For example, an AI-driven security system could analyze network traffic to detect unusual patterns that may indicate a cyberattack, and then take immediate action to block the threat and prevent further damage. This level of autonomous threat detection and response will be crucial for protecting sensitive data and ensuring the security of critical systems.

The ability of AI to handle massive amounts of data will be a game-changer. By 2025, AI will be able to process millions of tokens of information in a single context window, enabling it to carry out far more intricate tasks, like long-term planning, strategic decision-making, and complex problem-solving. The implications for business intelligence, operational efficiency, and personalized customer experiences will be vast, making AI an indispensable tool for organizations.

Main Applications of Frontier AI Use Cases

The potential applications of frontier AI use cases are both broad and transformative, spanning a wide range of industries and functions. Below are some of the key areas where frontier AI is expected to make a significant impact:

1. Customer Service: In customer service, AI will take on a far more personalized role, not just responding to customer inquiries

but predicting needs and offering tailored solutions. For example, an AI-driven customer service system could analyze a customer's purchase history and browsing behavior to predict their needs and offer personalized recommendations before the customer even makes a request. This level of proactive service will transform the customer experience, making it more seamless and satisfying.

2. Information Technology (IT): AI-driven IT systems will power smarter, more efficient networks, eliminating downtime and preemptively solving problems. For instance, an AI system could monitor network traffic and predict potential

bottlenecks, making adjustments to optimize performance before any issues arise. This capability will be particularly valuable in industries that rely on high-performance IT infrastructure, such as finance, healthcare, and e-commerce.

3. Cybersecurity: In cybersecurity, AI will act as a 24/7 sentinel, identifying and responding to threats in real-time, even as those threats evolve. For example, an AI-driven security system could analyze network traffic to detect unusual patterns that may indicate a cyberattack, and then take immediate action to block the threat and prevent further damage. This level of autonomous threat detection

and response will be crucial for protecting sensitive data and ensuring the security of critical systems.

4. Healthcare: In the healthcare industry, AI will be deployed for predictive analytics, streamlining operations, optimizing supply chains, and even detecting potential medical conditions before they manifest. For example, an AI system could analyze patient data to predict the likelihood of a disease and recommend preventive measures. This capability will enable healthcare providers to offer more personalized and proactive care, improving patient outcomes and reducing healthcare costs.

5. Finance: In the finance industry, AI will be used for predictive analytics, fraud detection, and portfolio management. For example, an AI system could analyze market data to predict trends and recommend investment strategies. Additionally, AI could be used to detect fraudulent activities by analyzing transaction patterns and identifying suspicious behavior. This will enable financial institutions to make more informed decisions, reduce risk, and enhance customer trust.

6. Manufacturing: In the manufacturing sector, AI will be used to optimize production processes, predict equipment failures, and improve supply chain management. For

example, an AI system could monitor equipment performance and predict maintenance needs, reducing downtime and improving efficiency. Additionally, AI could be used to optimize supply chains by predicting demand fluctuations and adjusting inventory levels accordingly.

7. Retail: In the retail industry, AI will enhance the shopping experience by providing personalized recommendations and optimizing inventory management. For example, an AI system could analyze a customer's purchase history and preferences to suggest products they are likely to buy. Additionally, AI could be used to monitor inventory levels and predict demand

fluctuations, ensuring that products are always in stock.

8. Energy and Utilities: In the energy and utilities sector, AI will be used to optimize energy consumption, predict equipment failures, and manage renewable energy sources. For example, an AI system could analyze data from smart meters to identify patterns in energy usage and suggest ways to reduce consumption. Additionally, AI could be used to predict fluctuations in energy production from renewable sources, ensuring a stable supply of electricity.

Challenges Ahead

While the promise of frontier AI use cases is immense, several challenges lie ahead. These challenges span technical, ethical, and operational domains and require a holistic approach to overcome.

1. Ethical Use of AI: The most pressing issue will be ensuring the ethical use of AI, particularly when it comes to handling sensitive data. AI systems will be processing vast amounts of information, which will raise concerns about privacy and data security. Organizations will need to develop robust governance structures to ensure that AI systems operate transparently and ethically.

2. Bias in AI Systems: Another challenge is the potential for bias in

AI systems. As AI becomes more autonomous, it will become increasingly important to ensure that it does not perpetuate or exacerbate existing biases in data or decision-making. Continued research into fairness, transparency, and accountability will be critical.

3. Computational Demands: The computational demands of frontier AI systems—especially as models grow in size and complexity—will present a significant challenge. Ensuring these systems are scalable, efficient, and sustainable will require new approaches to hardware, software, and energy consumption.

4. Integration with Existing Systems: Combining AI systems with current

infrastructure and workflows can be difficult, particularly in sectors reliant on outdated or legacy technologies. Ensuring that AI systems can seamlessly interact with these systems and that they do not disrupt existing workflows will be crucial for their successful implementation.

5. Regulation and Governance: As AI systems become more prevalent, there will be a need for clear regulations and governance frameworks to ensure their responsible use. This includes defining the roles and responsibilities of AI systems, establishing standards for their development and deployment, and

creating mechanisms for accountability.

6. Human-AI Collaboration: While AI systems are designed to operate autonomously, there will still be a need for human oversight and collaboration. Ensuring that humans and AI systems can work together effectively will be crucial for maximizing the benefits of this technology.

The Future of Frontier AI Use Cases

The future of frontier AI use cases is incredibly promising, with the potential to transform industries and solve some of the world's most complex problems. As AI systems become more autonomous and adaptable, they will be able to handle tasks that were once thought to be the exclusive domain of humans. This will lead to increased efficiency, improved decision-making, and new opportunities for innovation.

One of the most exciting prospects for frontier AI use cases is their ability to enable cross-domain collaboration. For example, an AI system in healthcare could share insights with an AI system in finance to develop personalized health insurance plans. Similarly, an AI system in logistics could collaborate with an AI system in manufacturing to optimize supply chains. This cross-domain collaboration will enable AI systems to tackle complex, multi-faceted problems that require a holistic approach.

Another key trend in the future of frontier AI use cases is the development of self-learning systems. These systems will be able to learn from their experiences and improve their performance over time, without requiring explicit programming. This will enable AI systems to adapt to new challenges and environments, making them even more versatile and powerful.

As AI systems become more prevalent, there will also be a growing need for interdisciplinary collaboration. Experts in fields such as computer science, ethics, law, and sociology will need to work together to address the challenges associated with AI systems and ensure that they are used in a way that benefits society. A comprehensive strategy is essential, one that addresses not just the technicaFor instance, an AI system might evaluate a customer's past purchases and online activity to recommend items they are probable to purchase.

In conclusion, frontier AI use cases represent the next wave of AI innovation, where systems operate with a level of sophistication and autonomy that was previously unimaginable. These use cases are transforming industries by enabling proactive problem-solving, enhancing customer experiences, and improving operational efficiency. While there are challenges that need to be addressed, the benefits of frontier AI use cases far outweigh the risks. By developing AI systems that are transparent, adaptable, and ethical, we can harness the full potential of this technology and create a better future for all.

2. Hybrid Augmented Intelligence: Enhancing Human Decision-Making with AI

What is Hybrid Augmented Intelligence?

Hybrid Augmented Intelligence represents a collaborative integration of artificial intelligence (AI) into human workflows to enhance—rather than replace—human decision-making. In this model, AI serves as a powerful tool that augments human expertise by offering insights, data-driven recommendations, and advanced analytical capabilities. However, the human retains ultimate control, applying emotional intelligence, creativity, and contextual understanding to make final judgments.

This approach thrives in fields requiring complex decision-making and nuanced interpretation, where full AI autonomy remains impractical.

The concept of Hybrid Augmented Intelligence is rooted in the idea that AI and humans each have unique strengths that, when combined, can lead to better outcomes than either could achieve alone. AI excels at processing vast amounts of data, identifying patterns, and making predictions with high accuracy. Humans, on the other hand, bring emotional intelligence, creativity, and the ability to understand context and make judgments based on experience and intuition. By leveraging the strengths of both, Hybrid Augmented Intelligence aims to create a synergistic relationship where AI enhances human decision-making without overshadowing it.

Healthcare serves as a prime example of Hybrid Augmented Intelligence in action. AI excels at analyzing medical images, diagnosing conditions, and suggesting treatment plans. Yet, human insight is essential for interpreting results within patient-specific contexts. For instance, an AI system might analyze a patient's medical history and suggest a treatment plan, but a doctor would consider the patient's unique circumstances, such as their lifestyle, preferences, and emotional state, before making a final decision. This collaboration ensures that AI supports rather than overshadows human expertise, leading to better patient outcomes.

The challenge lies in designing AI systems that seamlessly complement human capabilities without introducing friction or redundancy. Early studies have revealed that while AI outperformed doctors in isolated clinical reasoning tasks, performance dropped when human oversight was added without clear integration protocols. This underscores the essence of Hybrid Augmented Intelligence: achieving synergy where AI's computational strengths enhance human judgment, rather than complicating it. The true potential of this collaboration lies in refining how humans and AI interact to optimize outcomes across diverse domains.

The Evolution of Hybrid Augmented Intelligence in 2025

By 2025, Hybrid Augmented Intelligence systems will reach new levels of sophistication, enabling seamless collaboration between humans and AI across various industries. Significant advancements in user interface design will make AI tools more intuitive and user-friendly, empowering professionals to leverage AI capabilities without requiring deep technical expertise. AI will move beyond simply providing data or recommendations; it will actively assist humans in making better-informed decisions by identifying patterns, predicting outcomes, and suggesting alternative strategies in real-time.

Industries such as healthcare, law, and finance will experience deeper integration of AI into daily workflows. For instance, AI will support medical professionals by analyzing complex patient data and proposing potential diagnoses, while doctors will retain final decision-making authority, incorporating patient context, experience, and judgment. In this role, AI will function as an intelligent assistant, enhancing rather than replacing human expertise.

The advancement of Explainable AI (XAI) will be instrumental in this evolution, offering transparency into AI's reasoning processes and building trust among professionals. By 2025, professionals will feel more confident relying on AI for critical tasks, understanding not just the outcomes but also the rationale behind AI-generated insights. This clarity will empower them to make informed adjustments and decisions, ensuring a harmonious balance between human intuition and AI precision.

In healthcare, AI systems will analyze patient data, suggest diagnoses, and recommend treatment plans, but doctors will have the final say, considering the patient's unique circumstances. In law, AI will assist lawyers by analyzing legal documents, identifying relevant case law, and suggesting legal strategies, while lawyers will use their judgment to make final decisions. In finance, AI will analyze market data, predict trends, and recommend investment strategies, but financial advisors will consider their clients' goals and risk tolerance before making final recommendations.

The integration of AI into these industries will lead to more efficient workflows, better decision-making, and improved outcomes. However, achieving this level of integration will require addressing several challenges, including ensuring the integrity and fairness of AI outputs, building trust in AI systems, and designing intuitive user interfaces.

Main Applications of Hybrid Augmented Intelligence

The potential applications of Hybrid Augmented Intelligence are vast and transformative, spanning a wide range of industries and functions. Below are some of the key areas where Hybrid Augmented Intelligence is expected to make a significant impact:

1. Healthcare: In healthcare, Hybrid Augmented Intelligence will enhance patient care by combining the analytical capabilities of AI with the expertise of medical professionals. AI systems will analyze patient data, suggest diagnoses, and recommend treatment plans, while doctors will use their judgment to make final decisions. This collaboration will lead to more accurate diagnoses, personalized treatment plans, and better patient outcomes.

2. Law: In the legal industry, Hybrid Augmented Intelligence will assist lawyers by analyzing legal documents, identifying relevant case law, and suggesting legal strategies. Lawyers will use their judgment to

make final decisions, ensuring that the legal strategies are tailored to the specific needs of their clients. This collaboration will lead to more efficient legal research, better case preparation, and improved outcomes for clients.

3. Finance: In finance, Hybrid Augmented Intelligence will assist financial advisors by analyzing market data, predicting trends, and recommending investment strategies. Financial advisors will consider their clients' goals and risk tolerance before making final recommendations. This collaboration will lead to more informed investment decisions, better portfolio management, and

improved financial outcomes for clients.

4. Manufacturing: In the manufacturing sector, Hybrid Augmented Intelligence will optimize production processes by combining the analytical capabilities of AI with the expertise of human operators. AI systems will monitor equipment performance, predict maintenance needs, and suggest process improvements, while human operators will use their judgment to make final decisions. This collaboration will lead to more efficient production processes, reduced downtime, and improved product quality.

5. Customer Service: In customer service, Hybrid Augmented Intelligence will enhance the customer experience by combining the analytical capabilities of AI with the expertise of human agents. AI systems will analyze customer data, suggest solutions to common issues, and recommend personalized offers, while human agents will use their judgment to make final decisions. This collaboration will lead to more efficient customer service, higher customer satisfaction, and improved customer retention.

6. Education: In education, Hybrid Augmented Intelligence will enhance the learning experience by combining the analytical capabilities

of AI with the expertise of human teachers. AI systems will analyze student data, suggest personalized learning plans, and recommend teaching strategies, while teachers will use their judgment to make final decisions. This collaboration will lead to more personalized learning experiences, improved student outcomes, and more effective teaching strategies.

7. Creative Industries: In creative industries, Hybrid Augmented Intelligence will enhance the creative process by combining the analytical capabilities of AI with the creativity of human artists. AI systems will analyze creative works, suggest new ideas, and recommend creative

strategies, while artists will use their judgment to make final decisions. This collaboration will lead to more innovative creative works, improved artistic outcomes, and more effective creative processes.

Challenges Ahead

Despite its vast potential, Hybrid Augmented Intelligence faces several significant challenges. These challenges span technical, ethical, and operational domains and require a holistic approach to overcome.

1. Decision Paralysis: One key issue is the risk of overwhelming users with excessive data or too many recommendations, which can lead to decision paralysis. To address this, AI systems must be designed to filter

and prioritize information effectively, presenting only the most relevant insights. Intuitive and streamlined user interfaces will also be essential to ensure accessibility and ease of use.

2. Bias in AI Outputs: Another critical challenge lies in ensuring the integrity and fairness of AI outputs. AI systems can unintentionally inherit biases from their training data, subtly influencing outcomes in ways that may not be immediately apparent. Continuous monitoring, auditing, and robust transparency mechanisms will be crucial to identifying and mitigating these biases.

3. Trust and Transparency: Trust remains a foundational barrier. If AI systems are not transparent or their decision-making processes are not easily understandable, professionals may hesitate to rely on them. Effective training programs and clear communication about how AI arrives at its conclusions will be vital for building trust and encouraging adoption.

4. Integration with Existing Systems: Integrating AI systems into existing workflows can be challenging, especially in industries with legacy systems. Ensuring that AI systems can seamlessly interact with these systems and that they do not disrupt

existing workflows will be crucial for their successful implementation.

5. Regulation and Governance: As AI systems become more prevalent, there will be a need for clear regulations and governance frameworks to ensure their responsible use. This includes defining the roles and responsibilities of AI systems, establishing standards for their development and deployment, and creating mechanisms for accountability.

6. Human-AI Collaboration: While AI systems are designed to operate autonomously, there will still be a need for human oversight and collaboration. Ensuring that humans

and AI systems can work together effectively will be crucial for maximizing the benefits of this technology.

The Future of Hybrid Augmented Intelligence

The future of Hybrid Augmented Intelligence is incredibly promising, with the potential to transform industries and solve some of the world's most complex problems. As AI systems become more autonomous and adaptable, they will be able to handle tasks that were once thought to be the exclusive domain of humans. This will lead to increased efficiency, improved decision-making, and new opportunities for innovation.

One of the most exciting prospects for Hybrid Augmented Intelligence is its ability to enable cross-domain collaboration. For example, an AI system in healthcare could share insights with an AI system in finance to develop personalized health insurance plans. Similarly, an AI system in logistics could collaborate with an AI system in manufacturing to optimize supply chains. This cross-domain collaboration will enable AI systems to tackle complex, multi-faceted problems that require a holistic approach.

Another key trend in the future of Hybrid Augmented Intelligence is the development of self-learning systems. These systems will be able to learn from their experiences and improve their performance over time, without requiring explicit programming.

This will enable AI systems to adapt to new challenges and environments, making them even more versatile and powerful.

As AI systems with Hybrid Augmented Intelligence become more prevalent, there will also be a growing need for interdisciplinary collaboration. Experts in fields such as computer science, ethics, law, and sociology will need to work together to address the challenges associated with AI systems and ensure that they are used in a way that benefits society. A comprehensive strategy is essential, one that addresses not just the technicaFor instance, an AI system might evaluate a customer's past purchases and online activity to recommend items they are probable to purchase.

In conclusion, Hybrid Augmented Intelligence represents a significant leap forward in AI capabilities, enabling systems to enhance human decision-making without overshadowing it. This approach combines the strengths of AI and humans, leading to better outcomes across diverse domains. While there are challenges that need to be addressed, the benefits of Hybrid Augmented Intelligence far outweigh the risks. By developing AI systems that are transparent, adaptable, and ethical, we can harness the full potential of this technology and create a better future for all.

3. AI and Quantum Computing Convergence: The Future of Computational Power

What is AI and Quantum Computing Convergence?

The convergence of artificial intelligence (AI) and quantum computing represents one of the most groundbreaking advancements in technology. This fusion leverages the unique properties of quantum mechanics to enhance the capabilities of AI, enabling it to solve problems that are beyond the reach of classical computers. Quantum computing operates on the principles of quantum bits (qubits), which can exist in multiple states simultaneously, unlike classical bits that are either 0 or 1. This allows quantum computers to process vast amounts of data simultaneously, solving complex problems exponentially faster and more accurately than classical systems.

AI, on the other hand, excels at analyzing massive datasets, recognizing complex patterns, and making predictions. However, traditional computers often struggle with the sheer scale of data and optimization problems. Quantum computing can address these limitations by providing the computational power needed to handle large-scale data analysis and complex simulations. When combined, AI and quantum computing have the potential to revolutionize industries by vastly improving the speed, efficiency, and precision of data analysis, pattern recognition, and decision-making.

The synergy between AI and quantum computing could dramatically accelerate machine learning models, enabling AI to analyze more extensive datasets, refine its predictions, and generate more accurate insights. This is particularly valuable in fields that require complex simulations or optimization, such as drug discovery, financial modeling, and materials science. By harnessing the power of quantum computing, AI can achieve breakthroughs that were previously unattainable, opening new frontiers in technology and science.

The Evolution of AI and Quantum Computing Convergence in 2025

By 2025, the convergence between AI and quantum computing will shift from theoretical exploration to practical applications, with quantum-enhanced AI becoming a reality in specific domains. This evolution will be driven by advancements in quantum computing technology, the development of quantum algorithms, and the integration of quantum computing into existing AI frameworks.

In fields such as drug discovery, financial modeling, and materials science, quantum computing's ability to perform complex calculations will allow AI to run simulations and optimizations that were previously infeasible with classical computing. For example, in drug discovery, quantum AI could simulate molecular interactions with unprecedented accuracy, speeding up the process of finding new treatments. This capability will enable researchers to identify potential drug candidates more quickly and accurately, reducing the time and cost associated with drug development.

In financial markets, quantum-powered AI algorithms will be able to predict market shifts, optimize investment strategies, and perform risk assessments far more efficiently than current models. Quantum AI can analyze vast amounts of financial data, identify patterns, and make predictions with greater precision, enabling financial institutions to make more informed decisions and manage risks more effectively.

The integration of quantum computing will also address many of the current bottlenecks in AI's ability to process large datasets, optimize models, and handle computationally intensive tasks. Quantum AI will be particularly useful for solving high-dimensional problems, where the vast number of variables makes traditional methods impractical. This will open new frontiers in fields like machine learning itself, cryptography, and predictive analytics.

Main Applications of AI and Quantum Computing Convergence

The potential applications of AI and quantum computing convergence are vast and transformative, spanning a wide range of industries and functions. Below are some of the key areas where this convergence is expected to make a significant impact:

1. Cryptography: Quantum computing holds the promise of transforming the field of cryptography. While quantum computers could crack existing encryption methods, they will also be able to develop stronger, quantum-resistant encryption algorithms. This will enhance the security of digital communications and protect sensitive information from cyber threats. Quantum AI can be used to develop and test new cryptographic protocols, ensuring that they are secure against both classical and quantum attacks.

2. Drug Discovery: In drug discovery, AI powered by quantum computing will simulate molecular structures and interactions at a level of precision

that will significantly shorten drug development cycles and improve the accuracy of treatments. Quantum AI can analyze the complex interactions between molecules, predict the efficacy of potential drug candidates, and identify new therapeutic targets. This capability will accelerate the discovery of new drugs and improve the success rate of clinical trials.

3. Financial Modeling: In finance, quantum-enhanced AI will optimize portfolios, predict market movements, and manage financial risks with greater precision than traditional models. Quantum AI can analyze vast amounts of financial data, identify patterns, and make predictions with greater accuracy,

enabling financial institutions to make more informed decisions and manage risks more effectively. This will lead to more efficient financial markets and better investment outcomes.

4. Supply Chain Management: In supply chain management, quantum AI will optimize logistics, forecast demand, and streamline operations, reducing costs and improving efficiency. Quantum AI can analyze complex supply chain networks, identify bottlenecks, and optimize routes and inventory levels. This will enable companies to reduce costs, improve delivery times, and enhance customer satisfaction.

5. Materials Science: In materials science, quantum AI will enable the discovery and design of new materials with unique properties. Quantum AI can simulate the behavior of materials at the atomic level, predict their properties, and identify new materials for specific applications. This will accelerate the development of new materials for use in industries such as electronics, energy, and manufacturing.

6. Machine Learning: Quantum AI will revolutionize machine learning by enabling the development of more powerful and efficient algorithms. Quantum AI can handle high-dimensional data and complex optimization problems, making it

possible to train more accurate and robust machine learning models. This will lead to advancements in areas such as natural language processing, computer vision, and predictive analytics.

7. Predictive Analytics: In predictive analytics, quantum AI will enable the analysis of large and complex datasets, leading to more accurate predictions and insights. Quantum AI can identify patterns and trends in data that are not apparent with classical methods, enabling organizations to make more informed decisions and improve their operations.

Challenges Ahead

Despite the immense potential of AI and quantum computing convergence, several significant challenges need to be addressed to ensure its successful implementation. These challenges span technical, ethical, and operational domains and require a holistic approach to overcome.

1. Quantum Computing Technology: Quantum computing technology is still in its infancy, and current quantum machines lack the power and stability needed to handle large-scale applications. Quantum computers are extremely vulnerable to external environmental interference, which can lead to inaccuracies in their computational processes. Developing more stable and reliable quantum computers will be crucial for

realizing the full potential of quantum AI.

2. Quantum Algorithms: The development of quantum algorithms that can fully leverage quantum computing's capabilities is still in its early stages. These algorithms must be fine-tuned to ensure they provide practical advantages over classical systems. Researchers need to develop new quantum algorithms that are specifically designed for AI applications, such as machine learning and optimization.

3. Integration with Existing AI Frameworks: Integrating quantum computing into existing AI frameworks is a significant challenge. Quantum computers

require entirely new programming paradigms, and adapting current AI models to quantum environments will require collaboration between quantum physicists and AI experts. Developing tools and frameworks that facilitate the integration of quantum computing into AI workflows will be essential.

4. Accessibility and Cost: Quantum computing is resource-intensive and costly, which may limit its availability to large corporations and research institutions. Ensuring broader access to quantum AI tools, or creating hybrid systems that leverage both classical and quantum computing, will be crucial for democratizing its benefits. Developing cost-effective

quantum computing solutions and making them accessible to a wider range of users will be a key challenge.

5. Ethical and Security Concerns: The convergence of AI and quantum computing raises ethical and security concerns. Quantum AI has the potential to crack existing encryption methods, which could compromise the security of digital communications. Ensuring that quantum AI is used responsibly and that new quantum-resistant encryption methods are developed will be crucial for maintaining digital security.

6. Interdisciplinary Collaboration: The successful implementation of

quantum AI will require collaboration between experts in quantum physics, computer science, AI, and other fields. Developing a shared understanding of the challenges and opportunities associated with quantum AI will be essential for driving innovation and overcoming technical barriers.

The Future of AI and Quantum Computing Convergence

The future of AI and quantum computing convergence is incredibly promising, with the potential to transform industries and solve some of the world's most complex problems. As quantum computing technology matures and becomes more accessible, the integration of quantum computing into AI workflows will enable breakthroughs that were previously unattainable.

One of the most exciting prospects for quantum AI is its ability to enable cross-domain collaboration. For example, quantum AI could be used to simulate complex biological systems, leading to new insights in drug discovery and personalized medicine. Similarly, quantum AI could optimize supply chain networks, leading to more efficient and sustainable logistics.

Another key trend in the future of quantum AI is the development of hybrid systems that leverage both classical and quantum computing. These systems will combine the strengths of classical and quantum computing, enabling organizations to tackle complex problems more effectively.

For example, a hybrid system could use classical computing for data preprocessing and quantum computing for complex optimization tasks.

As quantum AI becomes more prevalent, there will also be a growing need for interdisciplinary collaboration. Experts in quantum physics, computer science, AI, and other fields will need to work together to address the challenges associated with quantum AI and ensure that it is used in a way that benefits society. This will require a holistic approach that considers not only the technical aspects of quantum AI but also its social and ethical implications.

In conclusion, the convergence of AI and quantum computing represents a significant leap forward in computational power, enabling the development of more powerful and efficient AI systems. While there are challenges that need to be addressed, the benefits of quantum AI far outweigh the risks. By developing quantum AI systems that are stable, reliable, and accessible, we can harness the full potential of this technology and create a better future for all.

4. Near Infinite Memory: The Future of AI Personalization and Contextual Understanding

What is Near Infinite Memory?

Near infinite memory refers to an AI system's ability to retain a virtually limitless amount of information over extended periods, enabling it to recall past interactions, conversations, preferences, and historical data. Unlike current AI models, which often operate with limited memory and reset with each new session, near infinite memory allows AI to maintain a continuous, evolving relationship with the user. This capability transforms AI from a transactional tool into a long-term, personalized assistant that grows smarter and more useful over time.

With near infinite memory, AI systems can remember a user's previous requests, preferences, and even their tone or mood, allowing them to offer more personalized, context-aware responses. For example, a customer support bot equipped with near infinite memory could recall a user's past issues, preferences, and resolutions, ensuring that each new interaction is more fluid and tailored to their specific needs. Similarly, a healthcare assistant could track a patient's medical history, providing personalized recommendations based on past treatments and continuously updating its advice as new information becomes available.

The concept of near infinite memory represents a significant leap forward in AI capabilities. It enables AI systems to move beyond reactive responses and into proactive assistance, offering deeper insights and more meaningful interactions. This shift has the potential to revolutionize industries by creating more intuitive, efficient, and human-like experiences.

The Evolution of Near Infinite Memory in 2025

By 2025, the concept of near infinite memory will transition from a futuristic idea to a practical reality. AI systems across various sectors, including customer service, healthcare, education, and beyond, will be equipped with the ability to remember and process long-term data. These systems will provide more than just reactive responses; they will anticipate needs, offer personalized advice, and make connections across past interactions, creating a more seamless and efficient user experience.

In customer service, AI with near infinite memory will remember past issues and interactions, allowing agents to offer more effective, tailored support. For example, if a customer has previously contacted support about a specific issue, the AI system will recall the details of that interaction and provide a more informed response, reducing the need for the customer to repeat themselves. This capability will enhance customer satisfaction and streamline support operations.

In healthcare, AI systems with near infinite memory will have access to a patient's entire medical history, enabling them to provide personalized care recommendations that are continuously updated as new information becomes available. For instance, an AI healthcare assistant could track a patient's medication history, allergies, and past treatments, offering tailored advice and reminders to ensure optimal care. This level of personalized support will improve patient outcomes and reduce the burden on healthcare providers.

Education will also benefit from AI systems with near infinite memory. These systems will track students' progress over time, adapting teaching methods and offering personalized feedback based on their learning history. For example, an AI tutor could remember a student's strengths and weaknesses, tailoring lessons to address areas where the student needs improvement. This personalized approach will enhance the learning experience and help students achieve their full potential.

With near infinite memory, AI will be able to proactively suggest actions, automate tasks, and offer advice based on a deep understanding of past interactions. This capability will enable AI to take on more complex roles, such as managing long-term projects, making strategic decisions, and offering insights that evolve over time. For example, an AI project management assistant could remember the details of a project from its inception, tracking progress, identifying potential issues, and offering recommendations to keep the project on track.

Main Applications of Near Infinite Memory

The potential applications of near infinite memory are vast and transformative, spanning a wide range of industries and functions. Below are some of the key areas where near infinite memory is expected to make a significant impact:

1. Customer Support: In customer support, AI systems with near infinite memory will provide a seamless, personalized experience by retaining a complete history of customer interactions and preferences. For example, a customer support bot could remember a user's past issues, preferences, and resolutions, ensuring that each new interaction is more fluid and tailored to their specific needs. This capability will

enhance customer satisfaction and streamline support operations.

2. Healthcare: In healthcare, AI systems with near infinite memory will offer continuous care by tracking medical histories and providing real-time treatment recommendations. For instance, an AI healthcare assistant could track a patient's medication history, allergies, and past treatments, offering tailored advice and reminders to ensure optimal care. This level of personalized support will improve patient outcomes and reduce the burden on healthcare providers.

3. Education: In education, AI tutors with near infinite memory will track student progress over time, adapting

teaching methods and offering personalized feedback based on their learning history. For example, an AI tutor could remember a student's strengths and weaknesses, tailoring lessons to address areas where the student needs improvement. This personalized approach will enhance the learning experience and help students achieve their full potential.

4. E-commerce: In e-commerce, AI systems with near infinite memory will remember past behavior and preferences to make more relevant recommendations or predictions. For example, an AI system could analyze a customer's purchase history and browsing behavior to suggest products they are likely to

buy. This level of personalization will enhance the shopping experience and increase customer loyalty.

5. Finance: In finance, AI systems with near infinite memory will track past transactions and financial behavior to offer personalized advice and recommendations. For instance, an AI financial advisor could remember a user's investment history and risk tolerance, offering tailored investment strategies and financial planning advice. This capability will help users make more informed financial decisions and achieve their financial goals.

6. Creative Sectors: In creative sectors, AI systems with near infinite memory will remember past projects

and preferences to offer more relevant suggestions and insights. For example, an AI creative assistant could remember a writer's past work and style, offering tailored suggestions for new projects. This level of personalization will enhance the creative process and help artists achieve their vision.

7. Professional Assistance: Professionals will find AI assistants with near infinite memory indispensable, as these systems can track ongoing tasks, remember project details, and assist with long-term planning and decision-making. For example, an AI project management assistant could remember the details of a project

from its inception, tracking progress, identifying potential issues, and offering recommendations to keep the project on track.

Challenges Ahead

While the promise of near infinite memory is immense, several challenges need to be addressed to ensure its successful implementation. These challenges span technical, ethical, and operational domains and require a holistic approach to overcome.

1. Privacy Concerns: The most obvious concern with near infinite memory is privacy. As AI systems store vast amounts of personal data, users will need control over what information is retained and for how long. Ensuring that users have

transparency and control over their data will be crucial for maintaining trust. Organizations will need to develop robust data governance frameworks to ensure that AI systems operate transparently and ethically.

2. Ethical Use of Data: There will also be ethical concerns about how the information stored in near infinite memory is used. Ensuring that AI systems use this data responsibly and do not misuse it for unethical purposes will be critical. Organizations will need to establish clear guidelines and ethical standards for the use of near infinite memory in AI systems.

3. Bias in Data: Bias could become a bigger issue in systems with long-term memory. If an AI system recalls biased or incomplete data, it could lead to skewed decisions or inappropriate responses. Ongoing monitoring and refinement of how AI systems update and store memory will be essential to ensure that they make fair and unbiased decisions.

4. Computational Resources: The computational resources required to support near infinite memory will be substantial. Storing and processing large volumes of data, particularly in real-time, will raise concerns about scalability, energy consumption, and efficiency. Developers will need to find innovative solutions to ensure

that these systems are sustainable, cost-effective, and scalable.

5. Integration with Existing Systems: Integrating AI systems with near infinite memory into existing systems and processes can be challenging, especially in industries with legacy systems. Ensuring that AI systems can seamlessly interact with these systems and that they do not disrupt existing workflows will be crucial for their successful implementation.

6. Regulation and Governance: As AI systems with near infinite memory become more prevalent, there will be a need for clear regulations and governance frameworks to ensure their responsible use. This includes

defining the roles and responsibilities of AI systems, establishing standards for their development and deployment, and creating mechanisms for accountability.

7. Human-AI Collaboration: While AI systems with near infinite memory are designed to operate autonomously, there will still be a need for human oversight and collaboration. Ensuring that humans and AI systems can work together effectively will be crucial for maximizing the benefits of this technology.

The Future of Near Infinite Memory

The future of near infinite memory is incredibly promising, with the potential to transform industries and solve some of the world's most complex problems. As AI systems become more autonomous and adaptable, they will be able to handle tasks that were once thought to be the exclusive domain of humans. This will lead to increased efficiency, improved decision-making, and new opportunities for innovation.

One of the most exciting prospects for near infinite memory is its ability to enable cross-domain collaboration. For example, an AI system in healthcare could share insights with an AI system in finance to develop personalized health insurance plans. Similarly, an AI system in logistics could collaborate with an AI system in manufacturing to optimize supply chains. This cross-domain collaboration will enable AI systems to tackle complex, multi-faceted problems that require a holistic approach.

Another key trend in the future of near infinite memory is the development of self-learning systems. These systems will be able to learn from their experiences and improve their performance over time, without requiring explicit programming. This will enable AI systems to adapt to new challenges and environments, making them even more versatile and powerful.

As AI systems with near infinite memory become more prevalent, there will also be a growing need for interdisciplinary collaboration. Experts in fields such as computer science, ethics, law, and sociology will need to work together to address the challenges associated with AI systems and ensure that they are used in a way that benefits society. A comprehensive strategy is essential, one that addresses not just the technicaFor instance, an AI system might evaluate a customer's past purchases and online activity to recommend items they are probable to purchase.

In conclusion, near infinite memory represents a significant leap forward in AI capabilities, enabling systems to retain and process vast amounts of information over extended periods. This capability transforms AI from a transactional tool into a long-term, personalized assistant that grows smarter and more useful over time. While there are challenges that need to be addressed, the benefits of near infinite memory far outweigh the risks. By developing AI systems that are transparent, adaptable, and ethical, we can harness the full potential of this technology and create a better future for all.

Section 3: Ethical and Collaborative AI

1. Explainable AI (XAI) and AI Alignment: Building Transparent and Ethical AI Systems

Introduction

As artificial intelligence (AI) systems become increasingly integrated into our daily lives, the need for transparency, interpretability, and ethical alignment has never been more critical. Explainable AI (XAI) and AI Alignment are two interconnected concepts that address these concerns. XAI focuses on creating AI systems whose decision-making processes are interpretable and understandable by humans, while AI Alignment ensures that these systems operate in ways that are consistent with human values, ethics, and societal norms. Together, these principles aim to build trust, accountability, and fairness in AI technologies, ensuring that they benefit humanity without causing unintended harm.

By 2025 and beyond, the demand for transparent and ethical AI systems will grow exponentially as AI is deployed in high-stakes domains such as healthcare, finance, criminal justice, and autonomous systems. This section explores the importance of XAI and AI Alignment, their evolution, key applications, challenges, and the future of these critical fields.

What is Explainable AI (XAI)?

Explainable AI (XAI) involves the development of artificial intelligence systems that offer transparent and comprehensible reasoning behind their decisions and behaviors. Unlike traditional "black-box" AI models, which produce outputs without revealing their internal logic, XAI systems aim to make their decision-making processes transparent and interpretable. This transparency is essential for building trust, ensuring accountability, and enabling humans to validate, debug, and improve AI systems.

Key Principles of XAI

1. Interpretability: The ability of humans to understand how an AI system arrives at its decisions.

2. Transparency: The openness of an AI system's internal processes,

including its data sources, algorithms, and decision criteria.

3. Justifiability: The ability of an AI system to provide logical and evidence-based explanations for its outputs.

4. Actionability: The ability of users to act on the explanations provided by an AI system, such as correcting errors or refining inputs.

Why XAI Matters

- Trust: People tend to place greater trust in AI systems when they have a clear understanding of the decision-making processes involved.

- Accountability: Transparent AI systems enable stakeholders to identify and address errors, biases, or unethical behavior.

- Compliance: Many industries, such as healthcare and finance, require AI systems to comply with regulatory standards that mandate transparency and explainability.
- Human-AI Collaboration: XAI enables humans to work alongside AI systems more effectively, leveraging their strengths while mitigating their limitations.

What is AI Alignment?

AI Alignment refers to the process of ensuring that AI systems act in ways that are aligned with human values, ethics, and goals. This involves designing AI systems that not only perform tasks efficiently but also adhere to ethical principles, respect human rights, and avoid harmful outcomes.

AI Alignment is particularly important as AI systems become more autonomous and capable of making decisions with significant societal impact.

Key Principles of AI Alignment

1. Value Alignment: Ensuring that AI systems prioritize human values and ethical principles in their decision-making.

2. Robustness: Designing AI systems that behave predictably and reliably, even in uncertain or adversarial environments.

3. Safety: Preventing AI systems from causing harm, either intentionally or unintentionally.

4. Fairness: Ensuring that AI systems treat all individuals and groups

equitably, without bias or
discrimination.

Why AI Alignment Matters

- Ethical Responsibility: AI systems
  must respect human dignity, rights,
  and freedoms.

- Risk Mitigation: Misaligned AI
  systems could cause harm, such as
  biased decisions, privacy violations,
  or unintended consequences.

- Public Acceptance: AI technologies
  are more likely to be accepted and
  adopted if they are perceived as
  ethical and aligned with societal
  values.

The Evolution of XAI and AI Alignment

The fields of XAI and AI Alignment have evolved significantly in recent years, driven by advancements in AI research, growing public awareness, and increasing regulatory scrutiny. By 2025, these fields will continue to mature, with new techniques, frameworks, and standards emerging to address the challenges of transparency and ethical alignment.

Key Milestones in XAI and AI Alignment

- Early Developments: Early AI systems were often rule-based and relatively interpretable. However, the rise of machine learning and deep learning introduced complex models that were difficult to understand.

- Rise of Black-Box Models: The success of deep learning in tasks like image recognition and natural language processing led to the widespread adoption of black-box models, which prioritized performance over interpretability.

- Growing Demand for Transparency: As AI systems were deployed in high-stakes domains, the lack of transparency became a significant concern, leading to the development of XAI techniques.

- Ethical AI Movement: The AI Alignment movement gained momentum as researchers and policymakers recognized the need to ensure that AI systems align with human values and ethics.

The Future of XAI and AI Alignment (2025 and Beyond)

By the year 2025, Explainable AI (XAI) and AI Alignment are expected to become essential elements in the creation and implementation of AI technologies. Key trends include:

- Standardization: The development of industry standards and best practices for XAI and AI Alignment.

- Regulation: Increased regulatory oversight to ensure that AI systems are transparent, ethical, and aligned with societal values.

- Interdisciplinary Collaboration: Greater collaboration between AI researchers, ethicists, policymakers, and domain experts to address the challenges of XAI and AI Alignment.

Applications of XAI and AI Alignment

XAI and AI Alignment have far-reaching applications across industries, enabling the development of transparent, ethical, and trustworthy AI systems. Below are some of the key areas where these principles are making an impact:

1. Healthcare

- Diagnostics: Explainable AI (XAI) systems can provide detailed explanations of their diagnostic processes, allowing medical professionals to verify and rely on the insights generated by AI.

- Treatment Recommendations: AI systems aligned with medical ethics can recommend treatments that prioritize patient well-being and avoid harmful side effects.

- Clinical Trials: XAI can provide transparent explanations for AI-driven decisions in clinical trials, ensuring compliance with regulatory standards.

2. Finance

- Credit Scoring: XAI systems can explain the factors influencing credit decisions, reducing bias and ensuring fairness.
- Fraud Detection: AI systems aligned with ethical principles can detect fraudulent activity without violating privacy or discriminating against individuals.
- Investment Strategies: XAI can provide transparent explanations for AI-driven investment recommendations, enabling

investors to make informed decisions.

3. Criminal Justice

- Risk Assessment: XAI systems can explain how they assess the risk of reoffending, ensuring fairness and accountability in sentencing decisions.

- Bias Mitigation: AI Alignment can help reduce biases in predictive policing and other criminal justice applications.

4. Autonomous Systems

- Self-Driving Cars: XAI systems can explain their decision-making processes, such as why a car chose to brake or change lanes, enhancing safety and trust.

- Drones: AI Alignment ensures that drones operate in ways that respect privacy, safety, and ethical guidelines.

5. Customer Service

- Chatbots: Explainable AI (XAI) allows chatbots to offer transparent reasoning behind their answers, enhancing user confidence and overall satisfaction.
- Personalization: AI systems aligned with ethical principles can personalize recommendations without compromising user privacy or autonomy.

6. Education

- Adaptive Learning: XAI systems can explain how they tailor learning experiences to individual students, ensuring transparency and fairness.

- Grading: AI Alignment ensures that automated grading systems are unbiased and aligned with educational goals.

Challenges in XAI and AI Alignment

Despite their potential, XAI and AI Alignment face several significant challenges that must be addressed to ensure their successful implementation.

1. Complexity of AI Models

- Numerous advanced AI models, including deep neural networks, are inherently intricate and challenging to understand.Simplifying these models without sacrificing performance is a major challenge.

2. Bias and Fairness

- AI systems can inadvertently perpetuate or amplify biases present in their training data. Ensuring fairness and mitigating bias requires ongoing monitoring and intervention.

3. Ethical Dilemmas

- AI Alignment involves navigating complex ethical dilemmas, such as balancing competing values or prioritizing certain outcomes over others.

4. Scalability

- Developing XAI and AI Alignment techniques that scale to large, real-world systems is a significant technical challenge.

5. Human Understanding

- Even with explanations, humans may struggle to understand the intricacies of AI decision-making, particularly in highly technical domains.

6. Regulatory Compliance

- Ensuring that AI systems comply with evolving regulatory standards for transparency and ethics requires significant effort and resources.

The Future of XAI and AI Alignment

The future of XAI and AI Alignment is bright, with numerous opportunities for innovation and impact. By 2025 and beyond, these fields will play a central role in shaping the development and deployment of AI technologies.

Key Trends

- Explainable Deep Learning: Advances in explainable deep learning will make complex models more interpretable without sacrificing performance.

- Ethical AI Frameworks: The development of ethical AI frameworks will provide guidelines for aligning AI systems with human values and societal norms.

- Human-Centric AI: AI systems will increasingly prioritize human well-being, ensuring that they enhance rather than undermine human autonomy and dignity.

- Global Collaboration: International collaboration will be essential for addressing the global challenges of

XAI and AI Alignment, ensuring that AI technologies benefit all of humanity.

Conclusion

Explainable AI (XAI) and AI Alignment are critical to building transparent, ethical, and trustworthy AI systems. By ensuring that AI systems are interpretable and aligned with human values, we can harness the power of AI to solve complex problems, improve decision-making, and enhance quality of life. Achieving this goal, however, demands tackling substantial technical, ethical, and societal obstacles.Through collaboration, innovation, and a commitment to ethical principles, we can create a future where AI serves as a force for good, empowering humanity to achieve its full potential.

2. Federated Learning: Collaborative AI Training Across Decentralized Data Sources

Introduction

In the era of big data and artificial intelligence (AI), the ability to train robust and accurate machine learning models often hinges on access to vast amounts of data. However, traditional centralized approaches to data collection and model training raise significant concerns about privacy, security, and data ownership. Federated Learning (FL) has emerged as a groundbreaking solution to these challenges, enabling collaborative AI training across decentralized data sources without compromising privacy. By allowing data to remain on local devices or within secure environments, Federated Learning ensures that sensitive information is never shared or exposed, while still enabling the development of powerful AI models.

By 2025 and beyond, Federated Learning is poised to revolutionize industries such as healthcare, finance, telecommunications, and more, where data privacy and security are paramount. This section explores the principles of Federated Learning, its evolution, key applications, challenges, and the future of this transformative technology.

What is Federated Learning?

Federated Learning is a decentralized approach to machine learning that enables multiple parties (such as devices, organizations, or institutions) to collaboratively train a shared AI model without transferring or centralizing their data. Instead of sending raw data to a central server, each participant trains the model locally using their own data and shares only the model updates (e.g., gradients or weights) with a central coordinator. These updates are combined to enhance the global model, which is subsequently shared with all participants for additional training.

Key Principles of Federated Learning

1. Data Decentralization: Data remains on local devices or within secure environments, ensuring privacy and reducing the risk of data breaches.

2. Collaborative Training: Multiple participants contribute to training a shared model, leveraging the

collective knowledge of diverse datasets.

3. Privacy Preservation: Techniques such as encryption, differential privacy, and secure multi-party computation are used to protect sensitive information.

4. Efficiency: Federated Learning minimizes the need for large-scale data transfers, reducing bandwidth and storage requirements.

Why Federated Learning Matters

- Privacy Protection: Federated Learning ensures that sensitive data, such as medical records or financial transactions, never leaves its source.

- Regulatory Compliance: FL helps organizations comply with data protection regulations like GDPR and HIPAA by minimizing data sharing.

- Scalability: FL enables the training of AI models on massive, distributed datasets without the need for centralized infrastructure.

- Collaboration: FL fosters collaboration between organizations, enabling them to pool their resources and expertise while maintaining data sovereignty.

The Evolution of Federated Learning

Federated Learning has its roots in the growing need for privacy-preserving AI solutions. As concerns about data privacy and security intensified, researchers and industry leaders began exploring decentralized approaches to machine learning. The concept of Federated Learning was first introduced by Google in 2017 as a way to improve predictive text models on mobile devices without uploading user data to central servers.

Since then, Federated Learning has evolved rapidly, driven by advancements in distributed computing, cryptography, and AI algorithms. By 2025, FL is expected to become a mainstream approach to AI training, with widespread adoption across industries.

Key Milestones in Federated Learning

- Early Research: Initial research focused on developing algorithms for decentralized training and aggregation, such as Federated Averaging (FedAvg).

- Industry Adoption: Companies like Google, Apple, and NVIDIA began implementing FL in applications such as keyboard predictions, healthcare analytics, and autonomous driving.
- Standardization: Efforts to standardize FL frameworks and protocols have gained momentum, enabling interoperability and scalability.
- Integration with Privacy Techniques: FL has been combined with privacy-preserving technologies like differential privacy and homomorphic encryption to enhance security.

The Future of Federated Learning (2025 and Beyond)

By 2025, Federated Learning will continue to evolve, with advancements in areas such as:

- Cross-Device and Cross-Silo FL: Expanding FL to include both edge devices (e.g., smartphones) and organizational silos (e.g., hospitals, banks).

- Federated Transfer Learning: Enabling knowledge transfer between different domains or tasks while preserving privacy.

- Federated Reinforcement Learning: Applying FL to reinforcement learning scenarios, such as robotics and autonomous systems.

- Federated Learning as a Service (FLaaS): Offering FL platforms and tools as cloud-based services to democratize access.

Applications of Federated Learning

Federated Learning has far-reaching applications across industries, enabling organizations to leverage the power of AI while preserving data privacy and security. Below are some of the key areas where FL is making an impact:

1. Healthcare

- Medical Diagnostics: Hospitals and clinics can collaboratively train AI models to diagnose diseases using patient data without sharing sensitive medical records.
- Drug Discovery: Pharmaceutical companies can pool data from clinical trials and research studies to

accelerate drug development while maintaining confidentiality.

- Personalized Medicine: Federated Learning (FL) facilitates the creation of customized treatment strategies by examining patient information from various sources while maintaining data privacy.

2. Finance

- Fraud Detection: Banks and financial institutions can train fraud detection models using transaction data from multiple sources without exposing customer information.

- Credit Scoring: FL allows lenders to improve credit scoring models by leveraging data from diverse populations while protecting individual privacy.

- Risk Management: Financial firms can use FL to analyze market trends and assess risks without sharing proprietary data.

3. Telecommunications

- Network Optimization: Telecom companies can use FL to optimize network performance by analyzing data from user devices without compromising privacy.
- Predictive Maintenance: FL enables the prediction of equipment failures by analyzing data from distributed sensors and devices.

4. Retail and E-Commerce

- Personalized Recommendations: Retailers can use FL to provide personalized product recommendations by analyzing user behavior across multiple platforms without sharing data.

- Inventory Management: FL helps retailers optimize inventory levels by analyzing sales data from multiple stores while maintaining data privacy.

5. Autonomous Systems

- Self-Driving Cars: Autonomous vehicle manufacturers can use FL to improve driving models by analyzing data from multiple vehicles without sharing sensitive location or sensor data.
- Smart Cities: FL enables the development of smart city applications, such as traffic management and energy

optimization, by analyzing data from distributed sensors and devices.

6. Education

- Adaptive Learning: FL allows educational institutions to develop personalized learning models by analyzing student data from multiple schools without compromising privacy.
- Research Collaboration: Researchers can use FL to collaborate on studies and share insights without exposing sensitive data.

Challenges in Federated Learning

Despite its potential, Federated Learning faces several significant challenges that must be addressed to ensure its successful implementation.

1. Communication Overhead

- FL requires frequent communication between participants and the central server, which can lead to high bandwidth and latency costs.

2. Data Heterogeneity

- Participants in FL often have non-IID (non-independent and identically distributed) data, which can make model training more challenging.

3. Privacy Risks

- While FL minimizes data sharing, there is still a risk of privacy breaches through model updates or inference attacks.

4. Model Aggregation

- Aggregating model updates from multiple participants while maintaining accuracy and fairness is a complex task.

5. Incentive Mechanisms

- Ensuring that participants are motivated to contribute to FL requires effective incentive mechanisms and fair reward systems.

6. Regulatory Compliance

- FL must comply with evolving data protection regulations, which can vary across regions and industries.

The Future of Federated Learning

The future of Federated Learning is bright, with numerous opportunities for innovation and impact. By 2025 and beyond, FL will play a central role in shaping the development and deployment of AI technologies.

Key Trends

- Edge AI Integration: FL will be increasingly integrated with edge computing, enabling real-time AI training on distributed devices.
- Privacy-Enhancing Technologies: FL will be combined with advanced privacy-preserving techniques, such as federated differential privacy and secure aggregation.
- Industry-Specific Solutions: FL will be tailored to meet the unique needs of industries such as healthcare, finance, and telecommunications.
- Global Collaboration: FL will foster global collaboration, enabling

organizations to pool their resources and expertise while maintaining data sovereignty.

Conclusion

Federated Learning represents a paradigm shift in AI training, enabling organizations to harness the power of decentralized data while preserving privacy and security. By 2025, FL will revolutionize industries, drive innovation, and empower individuals and organizations to collaborate on AI development without compromising data sovereignty. However, realizing this vision requires addressing significant technical, ethical, and regulatory challenges. Through collaboration, innovation, and a commitment to privacy and fairness, we can unlock the full potential of Federated

Learning and create a future where AI serves as a force for good, benefiting all of humanity.

3. AI Ethics and Governance: Ensuring Responsible AI Development

What is AI Ethics and Governance?

Artificial Intelligence (AI) has rapidly evolved from a theoretical concept to a transformative technology that permeates nearly every aspect of modern life. From healthcare and education to finance and transportation, AI systems are increasingly being deployed to make decisions, optimize processes, and even predict future outcomes. However, with this rapid advancement comes a host of ethical and governance challenges that must be addressed to ensure that AI is developed and deployed responsibly.

AI ethics refers to the moral principles and guidelines that govern the development, deployment, and use of AI technologies. It encompasses a wide range of considerations, including fairness, transparency, accountability, privacy, and the potential for bias and discrimination. AI governance, on the other hand, refers to the frameworks, policies, and regulations that are put in place to ensure that AI technologies are developed and used in a manner that aligns with societal values and ethical principles.

The importance of AI ethics and governance cannot be overstated. As AI systems become more autonomous and capable of making decisions that have significant impacts on individuals and society, it is crucial that these systems are designed and operated in a way that respects human rights, promotes fairness, and minimizes harm. Without proper ethical guidelines and governance structures, there is a risk that AI technologies could be used in ways that exacerbate existing inequalities, infringe on privacy, or even cause harm.

One of the key challenges in AI ethics and governance is the rapid pace of technological advancement. Unlike traditional technologies, which often evolve over decades, AI technologies can advance at an exponential rate, making it difficult for ethical guidelines and governance frameworks to keep up. This creates a situation where AI systems may be deployed before their ethical implications are fully understood, leading to potential risks and unintended consequences.

Another challenge is the global nature of AI development and deployment. AI technologies are often developed by multinational corporations and deployed across multiple countries, each with its own cultural, legal, and ethical norms. This creates a complex landscape where different jurisdictions may have different expectations and requirements for AI systems, making it difficult to establish a unified set of ethical guidelines and governance structures.

Despite these challenges, there is a growing recognition of the importance of AI ethics and governance. Governments, industry leaders, and civil society organizations are increasingly coming together to develop ethical guidelines and governance frameworks that can help ensure that AI technologies are developed and used in a responsible manner. These efforts are critical to building public trust in AI technologies and ensuring that they are used to benefit society as a whole.

Key Ethical Challenges in AI

As AI technologies become more pervasive, they raise a host of ethical challenges that must be addressed to ensure their responsible development and deployment. These challenges are multifaceted and often interrelated, requiring a holistic approach to AI ethics and governance. Below, we explore some of the key ethical challenges in AI, including bias and fairness, transparency and explainability, privacy and surveillance, accountability and responsibility, and the potential for job displacement and economic inequality.

1. Bias and Fairness

One of the most pressing ethical challenges in AI is the issue of bias and fairness. AI systems are often trained on large datasets that may contain biases, either explicit or implicit. These biases can be introduced at various stages of the AI development process, from data collection and labeling to model training and deployment. If not addressed, these biases can lead to unfair or discriminatory outcomes, particularly for marginalized or underrepresented groups.

For example, facial recognition systems have been shown to have higher error rates for people with darker skin tones, leading to concerns about racial bias. Similarly, AI systems used in hiring or lending decisions may inadvertently discriminate against certain groups if the training data reflects historical biases. Addressing these issues requires a concerted effort to identify and mitigate biases in AI systems, as well as ongoing monitoring and evaluation to ensure that AI systems remain fair and equitable over time.

2. Transparency and Explainability

Another key ethical challenge in AI is the need for transparency and explainability. Many AI systems, particularly those based on deep learning, operate as "black boxes," meaning that their decision-making processes are not easily understood by humans. This lack of transparency can make it difficult to assess whether an AI system is making fair and accurate decisions, and it can also make it challenging to hold AI systems accountable for their actions.

Explainability is particularly important in high-stakes applications, such as healthcare, criminal justice, and finance, where AI decisions can have significant impacts on individuals' lives. In these contexts, it is crucial that AI systems can provide clear and understandable explanations for their decisions, so that users can trust and verify the outcomes. Achieving this level of explainability is a complex technical challenge, but it is essential for building public trust in AI technologies.

3. Privacy and Surveillance

AI technologies have the potential to significantly impact privacy and surveillance. On one hand, AI can be used to enhance privacy by enabling more secure and efficient data protection mechanisms. On the other hand, AI can also be used to enable mass surveillance, where individuals' activities are monitored and analyzed on a large scale, often without their knowledge or consent.

The use of AI in surveillance raises significant ethical concerns, particularly when it comes to the potential for abuse by governments or corporations. For example, AI-powered surveillance systems could be used to track individuals' movements, monitor their online activities, or even predict their behavior based on past actions. This raises questions about the balance between security and privacy, and the extent to which individuals should have control over their personal data.

4. Accountability and Responsibility

As AI systems become more autonomous, questions of accountability and responsibility become increasingly complex. In traditional systems, humans are typically responsible for the decisions and actions taken by machines. However, as AI systems become more capable of making decisions on their own, it becomes less clear who should be held accountable when things go wrong.

For example, if an autonomous vehicle is involved in an accident, who is responsible—the manufacturer, the software developer, or the user? Similarly, if an AI system used in healthcare makes a wrong diagnosis, who should be held accountable—the developer, the healthcare provider, or the AI system itself? These questions are not just theoretical; they have real-world implications for how AI systems are regulated and how liability is assigned in cases of harm.

5. Job Displacement and Economic Inequality

The widespread adoption of AI technologies has the potential to significantly impact the labor market, leading to job displacement and economic inequality. AI systems are increasingly capable of performing tasks that were previously done by humans, from manufacturing and customer service to data analysis and decision-making. While this can lead to increased efficiency and productivity, it also raises concerns about the potential for job loss and the widening gap between those who have the skills to work with AI and those who do not.

The impact of AI on employment is likely to be uneven, with some industries and regions being more affected than others. For example, jobs that involve routine, repetitive tasks are more likely to be automated, while jobs that require creativity, empathy, and complex problem-solving are less likely to be affected. This could lead to significant economic disruption, particularly for workers in low-skilled or routine-based jobs.

Addressing these challenges requires a proactive approach to workforce development and education, as well as policies that support workers who are displaced by AI technologies. This could include initiatives such as retraining programs, universal basic income, and policies that promote the creation of new jobs in emerging industries.

Global AI Governance Frameworks and Regulations

As AI technologies continue to advance, there is a growing recognition of the need for global governance frameworks and regulations to ensure that AI is developed and used in a responsible and ethical manner. These frameworks are essential for addressing the ethical challenges outlined above, as well as for promoting international cooperation and coordination in the development and deployment of AI technologies.

1. National and Regional AI Strategies

Many countries and regions have developed their own AI strategies and governance frameworks to guide the development and deployment of AI technologies. These strategies often include a mix of regulatory measures, ethical guidelines, and investment in AI research and development.

For example, the European Union (EU) has been at the forefront of AI governance, with the development of the EU's AI Act, which aims to create a comprehensive regulatory framework for AI technologies. The AI Act categorizes AI systems based on their level of risk, with stricter regulations for high-risk applications such as healthcare, transportation, and law enforcement. The EU's approach emphasizes the importance of transparency, accountability, and human oversight in AI systems, and it includes provisions for the protection of fundamental rights and freedoms.

Similarly, the United States has developed a National AI Initiative, which includes a set of principles for the responsible development and use of AI technologies. These principles emphasize the importance of fairness, transparency, and accountability, as well as the need for public-private partnerships to advance AI research and development. The U.S. approach also includes a focus on workforce development and education, to ensure that workers are prepared for the changes brought about by AI technologies.

China, on the other hand, has taken a more centralized approach to AI governance, with the development of the New Generation

Artificial Intelligence Development Plan. This plan outlines a comprehensive strategy for the development of AI technologies, with a focus on achieving global leadership in AI by 2030. China's approach emphasizes the importance of innovation and technological advancement, as well as the need for ethical considerations in the development and deployment of AI technologies.

2. International Cooperation and Coordination

Given the global nature of AI development and deployment, international cooperation and coordination are essential for the development of effective AI governance frameworks. This includes efforts to harmonize regulations and standards across different jurisdictions, as well as initiatives to promote the sharing of best practices and knowledge.

One example of international cooperation in AI governance is the Global Partnership on

Artificial Intelligence (GPAI), which was launched in 2020 by a group of like-minded countries, including Canada, France, Germany, and the United States. The GPAI aims to promote the responsible development and use of AI technologies, with a focus on addressing key ethical and societal challenges. The partnership includes working groups on topics such as data governance, responsible AI, and the future of work, and it provides a platform for international collaboration and knowledge sharing.

Another example is the OECD's Principles on Artificial Intelligence, which were adopted in 2019 by the Organization for Economic Cooperation and Development (OECD). These principles provide a set of guidelines for the responsible development and use of AI technologies, with a focus on promoting inclusive growth, sustainable development, and human-centered values. The OECD principles have been endorsed by over 40 countries, making them a widely recognized framework for AI governance.

3. Ethical Guidelines and Standards

In addition to regulatory frameworks, there is also a growing body of ethical guidelines and standards for AI development and deployment. These guidelines are often developed by industry groups, academic institutions, and civil society organizations, and they provide a set of best practices for ensuring that AI technologies are developed and used in a responsible and ethical manner.

For example, the IEEE Global Initiative on Ethics of Autonomous and Intelligent Systems has developed a set of ethical guidelines for AI and autonomous systems, known as the Ethically Aligned Design (EAD) framework. The EAD framework provides a comprehensive set of principles and recommendations for the design, development, and deployment of AI systems, with a focus on promoting human well-being, fairness, and transparency.

Similarly, the Partnership on AI, which includes members from industry, academia, and civil society, has developed a set of best practices for AI development and deployment. These best practices emphasize the importance of fairness, accountability, and transparency, as well as the need for ongoing monitoring and evaluation of AI systems to ensure that they remain aligned with ethical principles.

4. The Role of Multinational Organizations in AI Governance

Multinational organizations play a critical role in the development and implementation of AI governance frameworks. These organizations, which include international bodies such as the United Nations (UN), the World Economic Forum (WEF), and the International

Telecommunication Union (ITU), provide a platform for global cooperation and coordination on AI governance issues.

The United Nations, for example, has been actively engaged in discussions on AI governance, with a focus on promoting the responsible development and use of AI technologies in support of the Sustainable Development Goals (SDGs). The UN has established a High-Level Panel on Digital Cooperation, which includes recommendations on AI governance, as well as initiatives to promote international cooperation on AI-related issues.

The World Economic Forum has also been a key player in AI governance, with the development of the AI Governance Toolkit, which provides a set of practical tools and resources for organizations to develop and implement AI governance frameworks. The WEF has also established the Global AI Council, which brings together leaders from industry, government, and civil society to promote the responsible development and use of AI technologies.

The International Telecommunication Union (ITU) has been working on AI governance through its AI for Good initiative, which aims to promote the use of AI technologies to address global challenges such as climate change, healthcare, and education. The ITU has also developed a set of AI ethics guidelines, which provide a framework for the responsible development and use of AI technologies.

5. The Future of Ethical AI Development

As AI technologies continue to evolve, the future of ethical AI development will depend on the ability of governments, industry, and civil society to work together to address the ethical challenges outlined above. This will require a continued focus on transparency, accountability, and fairness, as well as ongoing efforts to promote international cooperation and coordination on AI governance issues.

One key area of focus for the future of ethical AI development is the need for more robust and comprehensive regulatory frameworks. While many countries and regions have developed their own AI strategies and governance frameworks, there is still a need for greater harmonization and coordination across different jurisdictions. This will require ongoing efforts to develop international standards and guidelines for AI development and deployment, as well as initiatives to promote the sharing of best practices and knowledge.

Another key area of focus is the need for greater investment in AI research and development, particularly in areas such as explainability, fairness, and privacy. This will require collaboration between industry, academia, and government, as well as a commitment to funding research that addresses the ethical challenges of AI technologies.

Finally, the future of ethical AI development will depend on the ability of society to adapt to the changes brought about by AI technologies. This will require a focus on workforce development and education, as well as policies that support workers who are displaced by AI technologies. It will also require a commitment to promoting inclusive growth and sustainable development, to ensure that the benefits of AI technologies are shared by all.

In conclusion, AI ethics and governance are critical to ensuring that AI technologies are developed and used in a responsible and ethical manner. By addressing the key ethical challenges in AI, developing global governance frameworks and regulations, and promoting international cooperation and coordination, we can ensure that AI technologies are used to benefit society as a whole, while minimizing the risks and unintended consequences. The future of ethical AI development will depend on the ability of governments, industry, and civil society to work together to address these challenges and to promote the responsible development and use of AI technologies.

Section 4: AI in Industry and Society

1. AI in Healthcare: Revolutionizing Diagnosis, Treatment, and Drug Discovery

The healthcare sector is undergoing a significant transformation due to Artificial Intelligence (AI), which is unlocking new possibilities for enhancing diagnosis, treatment, and the development of medications. The integration of AI into healthcare is not just a technological advancement; it is a paradigm shift that has the potential to revolutionize how we understand and manage health and disease. This chapter explores the current applications of AI in healthcare, the rise of AI-powered personalized medicine, the challenges in adopting AI in healthcare, and the future prospects of AI in this critical field.

Current Applications of AI in Healthcare

AI is already making significant strides in various areas of healthcare, from diagnostics to treatment planning and administrative tasks. The following are some of the key applications of AI in healthcare today:

1. Medical Imaging and Diagnostics

One of the most significant uses of AI in healthcare is in the field of medical imaging and diagnostics. AI algorithms, particularly those based on deep learning, have shown remarkable accuracy in analyzing medical images such as X-rays, MRIs, and CT scans. These algorithms can detect abnormalities, such as tumors, fractures, and other conditions, often with a level of precision that rivals or even surpasses that of human radiologists.

For example, AI systems have been developed to detect breast cancer in mammograms, lung cancer in CT scans, and diabetic retinopathy in retinal images. These systems can analyze large volumes of images quickly, reducing the time required for diagnosis and allowing for earlier detection of diseases, which is critical for successful treatment.

2. Predictive Analytics and Risk Stratification

AI is also being used to predict patient outcomes and stratify risks based on historical data. By analyzing electronic health records (EHRs), AI algorithms can identify patterns and correlations that may not be apparent to human clinicians. This enables healthcare providers to predict which patients are at risk of developing certain conditions, such as heart disease, diabetes, or sepsis, and to intervene early to prevent or mitigate these conditions.

Predictive analytics can also be used to optimize hospital operations, such as predicting patient admission rates, bed occupancy, and staffing needs. This enables healthcare providers to distribute resources more effectively and enhance the quality of patient care.

3. Virtual Health Assistants and Chatbots

AI-driven virtual health assistants and chatbots are gaining widespread popularity in the healthcare sector. These tools can provide patients with instant access to medical information, answer questions about symptoms, and offer guidance on whether to seek medical attention. Virtual health assistants can also help patients manage chronic conditions by providing reminders to take medications, tracking symptoms, and offering lifestyle recommendations.

Chatbots are particularly useful in triaging patients, especially in situations where healthcare resources are limited. For example, during the COVID-19 pandemic, chatbots were used to screen patients for symptoms and provide guidance on testing and quarantine measures.

4. Drug Discovery and Development

AI is revolutionizing the drug discovery and development process, which has traditionally been time-consuming and expensive. AI algorithms can analyze vast amounts of biological and chemical data to identify potential drug candidates, predict their efficacy, and optimize their chemical structures. This speeds up the drug development process and lowers the expenses associated with introducing new medications to the market.

For example, AI has been used to identify potential treatments for diseases such as Alzheimer's, cancer, and COVID-19. In some cases, AI has identified existing drugs that could be repurposed for new indications, significantly reducing the time and cost of development.

5. Robotic Surgery and Assistance

AI is also being integrated into robotic surgery systems, enabling surgeons to perform complex procedures with greater precision and control. Robotic surgery systems, such as the da Vinci Surgical System, use AI algorithms to assist surgeons in real-time, providing enhanced visualization, precision, and dexterity. This minimizes the likelihood of complications and enhances patient results.

In addition to robotic surgery, AI-powered robotic assistants are being used in hospitals to perform tasks such as delivering medications, transporting supplies, and assisting with patient care. These robots can help reduce the workload on healthcare staff and improve the efficiency of hospital operations.

AI-Powered Personalized Medicine

Personalized medicine, often referred to as precision medicine, is a modern healthcare strategy that customizes medical treatments based on the unique attributes of each patient. AI is playing a crucial role in advancing personalized medicine by enabling the analysis of complex datasets, including genetic, clinical, and lifestyle data, to develop personalized treatment plans.

1. Genomic Medicine

AI is transforming genomic medicine by enabling the analysis of large-scale genomic data to identify genetic variants associated with diseases. This information can be used to predict an individual's risk of developing certain conditions and to guide personalized treatment decisions.

For example, AI algorithms have been used to analyze the genomes of cancer patients to identify mutations that drive tumor growth. This information can be used to select targeted therapies that are most likely to be effective for each patient, improving treatment outcomes and reducing the risk of side effects.

2. Predictive Modeling for Personalized Treatment

AI is also being used to develop predictive models that can guide personalized treatment decisions. These models analyze data from multiple sources, including EHRs, genomic data, and wearable devices, to predict how a patient is likely to respond to different treatments.

For example, AI algorithms have been developed to predict the likelihood of a patient responding to a specific cancer treatment based on their genetic profile and clinical history. This allows oncologists to select the most effective treatment for each patient, reducing the trial-and-error approach that is often used in cancer treatment.

3. Wearable Devices and Remote Monitoring

Wearable devices, such as smartwatches and fitness trackers, are increasingly being used to collect real-time health data, such as heart rate, blood pressure, and activity levels. AI algorithms can analyze this data to provide personalized health recommendations and to detect early signs of health issues.

For example, AI-powered wearable devices can monitor a patient's heart rate and detect irregularities that may indicate atrial fibrillation or other cardiac conditions. This allows for early intervention and can prevent serious complications.

Remote monitoring is particularly valuable for patients with chronic conditions, such as diabetes or hypertension, who require ongoing management. AI-powered remote monitoring systems can track patients' health metrics and provide alerts to healthcare providers if any abnormalities are detected, enabling timely interventions and reducing the need for hospital visits.

Challenges in AI Healthcare Adoption

Despite the significant potential of AI in healthcare, there are several challenges that must be addressed to ensure its successful adoption and integration into clinical practice.

These challenges include technical, ethical, regulatory, and organizational issues.

1. Data Quality and Availability

The performance of AI algorithms relies heavily on the volume and accuracy of data used for training and validation purposes.In healthcare, data is often fragmented, incomplete, or inconsistent, which can limit the performance of AI systems. Additionally, there are concerns about the representativeness of the data, as biases in the data can lead to biased AI models that may not perform well for all patient populations.

Ensuring data quality and availability requires significant investment in data infrastructure, including the development of standardized data formats, data sharing agreements, and data governance frameworks. It also requires collaboration between healthcare organizations, technology companies, and regulatory bodies to ensure that data is collected, stored, and used in a manner that protects patient privacy and confidentiality.

2. Ethical and Legal Considerations

The use of AI in healthcare raises several ethical and legal considerations, including issues related to patient consent, data privacy, and algorithmic bias. Patients must be informed about how their data will be used and must have the opportunity to opt out of data collection and analysis. Additionally, healthcare providers must ensure that AI systems are transparent and explainable, so that patients and clinicians can understand how decisions are made.

Algorithmic bias is another significant concern, as biased AI models can lead to unequal treatment of patients based on factors such as race, gender, or socioeconomic status. Addressing these issues requires ongoing monitoring and evaluation of AI systems, as well as the development of ethical guidelines and regulatory frameworks to ensure that AI is used in a fair and equitable manner.

3. Regulatory and Reimbursement Challenges

The regulatory landscape for AI in healthcare is still evolving, and there is a lack of clear guidelines on how AI-based medical devices and software should be evaluated and approved. Regulatory bodies, such as the U.S. Food and Drug Administration (FDA), are working to develop frameworks for the evaluation of AI technologies, but there is still uncertainty about how these frameworks will be implemented and enforced.

Reimbursement is another challenge, as healthcare providers may be reluctant to adopt AI technologies if they are not covered by insurance or if the cost of implementation is too high. Addressing these challenges requires collaboration between regulatory bodies, healthcare providers, and payers to develop reimbursement models that support the adoption of AI technologies.

4. Integration into Clinical Workflows

Integrating AI into clinical workflows can be challenging, as it requires changes to existing processes and practices. Healthcare providers may be resistant to adopting AI technologies if they perceive them as disruptive or if they lack the necessary training and support to use them effectively.

To overcome these challenges, healthcare organizations must invest in training and education to ensure that clinicians are comfortable using AI technologies. Additionally, AI systems must be designed with usability in mind, so that they can be easily integrated into existing workflows and provide value to clinicians and patients.

5. Trust and Acceptance

Trust plays a vital role in the acceptance and integration of AI within the healthcare sector. Patients and clinicians must trust that AI systems are accurate, reliable, and safe to use. Building trust requires transparency in how AI systems are developed and validated, as well as ongoing monitoring and evaluation to ensure that they continue to perform as expected.

Public acceptance of AI in healthcare is also important, as patients may be hesitant to accept AI-based diagnoses or treatments if they do not understand how the technology works. Educating patients and the public about the benefits and limitations of AI in healthcare is essential for building acceptance and trust.

The Future of AI in Healthcare

The future of AI in healthcare is promising, with the potential to transform every aspect of the healthcare system, from diagnosis and treatment to drug discovery and patient care. However, realizing this potential will require continued investment in research and development, as well as collaboration between stakeholders to address the challenges outlined above.

1. Advancements in AI Algorithms and Technologies

As AI algorithms and technologies continue to advance, we can expect to see even more sophisticated applications in healthcare. For example, the development of explainable AI (XAI) will enable clinicians to understand how AI systems arrive at their decisions, increasing trust and acceptance. Additionally, advancements in natural language processing (NLP) will enable AI systems to analyze unstructured data, such as clinical notes and medical literature, providing deeper insights into patient care.

2. Integration with Other Emerging Technologies

AI will increasingly be integrated with other emerging technologies, such as the Internet of Medical Things (IoMT), blockchain, and 5G networks. The IoMT, which includes connected medical devices and wearable technologies, will generate vast amounts of real-time health data that can be analyzed by AI systems to provide personalized health recommendations and early warnings of health issues.

Blockchain technology can be used to secure and share health data, ensuring that it is accurate, tamper-proof, and accessible to authorized parties. 5G networks will enable the rapid transmission of large datasets, supporting real-time AI applications such as remote surgery and telemedicine.

3. Expansion of AI in Global Health

AI has the potential to address some of the most pressing challenges in global health, particularly in low-resource settings where access to healthcare is limited. AI-powered diagnostic tools, such as smartphone-based imaging systems, can be used to provide affordable and accessible healthcare in remote and underserved areas. Additionally, AI can be used to analyze global health data to identify trends and predict outbreaks of infectious diseases, enabling timely interventions and resource allocation.

4. Ethical AI and Responsible Innovation

As AI becomes more integrated into healthcare, it will be essential to ensure that it is developed and used in an ethical and responsible manner. This will require ongoing collaboration between stakeholders to develop ethical guidelines, regulatory frameworks, and best practices for AI in healthcare. Additionally, it will be important to engage with patients and the public to ensure that AI technologies are aligned with societal values and priorities.

5. Personalized and Preventive Healthcare

The future of healthcare will be increasingly personalized and preventive, with AI playing a central role in enabling this shift. AI-powered predictive models will enable healthcare providers to identify individuals at risk of developing certain conditions and to intervene early to prevent or mitigate these conditions. Additionally, AI will enable the development of personalized treatment plans that are tailored to the unique characteristics of each patient, improving outcomes and reducing the risk of adverse effects.

In conclusion, AI is revolutionizing healthcare, offering unprecedented opportunities to improve diagnosis, treatment, and drug discovery. However, realizing the full potential of AI in healthcare will require addressing the challenges of data quality, ethical considerations, regulatory frameworks, and integration into clinical workflows. By investing in research and development, fostering collaboration between stakeholders, and ensuring that AI is developed and used in an ethical and responsible manner, we can unlock the transformative potential of AI in healthcare and improve the lives of patients around the world.

2. AI in Education: Transforming Learning and Skill Development

Artificial Intelligence (AI) is revolutionizing the field of education, offering new opportunities to enhance learning and skill development. From personalized learning systems to adaptive learning platforms, AI is transforming how students learn, how teachers teach, and how educational institutions operate. This chapter explores the role of AI in education, focusing on AI-powered personalized learning systems, applications of AI in remote and adaptive learning, challenges in implementing AI in education, and the future of AI-driven education.

AI-Powered Personalized Learning Systems

One of AI's most impactful advancements in education is the creation of tailored learning platforms. These systems leverage AI algorithms to tailor educational content and experiences to the individual needs, preferences, and learning styles of each student. By analyzing data on students' performance, engagement, and behavior,

AI-powered personalized learning systems can provide customized recommendations, feedback, and support, helping students to achieve their full potential.

1. Adaptive Learning Platforms

Adaptive learning platforms are a key application of AI in personalized learning. These platforms use AI algorithms to analyze students' interactions with educational content, such as quizzes, assignments, and reading materials, and to adjust the content in real-time based on their performance. For example, if a student is struggling with a particular concept, the platform may provide additional explanations, practice exercises, or alternative learning resources to help the student master the concept.

Adaptive learning platforms can also track students' progress over time, identifying areas where they may need additional support and providing targeted interventions. This personalized approach to learning helps to ensure that students are challenged at the right level and can progress at their own pace, leading to better learning outcomes.

2. Intelligent Tutoring Systems

Intelligent tutoring systems (ITS) are another important application of AI in personalized learning. These systems use AI to provide one-on-one tutoring to students, offering personalized instruction, feedback, and guidance. ITS can simulate the experience of working with a human tutor, providing explanations, answering questions, and offering hints and suggestions to help students solve problems.

For example, an ITS for mathematics might analyze a student's problem-solving process, identify errors or misconceptions, and provide targeted feedback to help the student correct their mistakes. The system can also adapt the difficulty of the problems based on the student's performance, ensuring that they are continually challenged and engaged.

3. Learning Analytics and Data-Driven Insights

AI-powered learning analytics tools are transforming how educators understand and support student learning. These tools analyze data from various sources, such as online learning platforms, assessments, and student interactions, to provide insights into students' learning behaviors, performance, and engagement.

For example, learning analytics can identify patterns in students' study habits, such as the times of day they are most active or the types of resources they prefer. This information can be used to provide personalized recommendations, such as suggesting study schedules or resources that align with the student's preferences and needs.

Learning analytics can also help educators identify at-risk students who may be struggling or disengaged. By providing early warnings and targeted interventions, educators can support these students and help them stay on track.

Applications of AI in Remote and Adaptive Learning

The COVID-19 pandemic has accelerated the adoption of remote and online learning, and AI is playing a crucial role in enabling these new modes of education. AI-powered tools and platforms are helping to make remote and adaptive learning more effective, engaging, and accessible.

1. Virtual Classrooms and Online Learning Platforms

AI is enhancing virtual classrooms and online learning platforms by providing features such as automated grading, real-time feedback, and personalized content recommendations. For example, AI-powered grading systems can automatically assess students' assignments and exams, providing instant feedback and reducing the workload for educators.

AI can also enhance the interactivity of virtual classrooms by enabling features such as real-time language translation, speech recognition, and sentiment analysis. These features can help to create a more inclusive and engaging learning environment, particularly for students who may be non-native speakers or have different learning needs.

2. AI-Powered Content Creation and Curation

AI is being used to create and curate educational content, making it easier for educators to develop high-quality learning materials. For example, AI-powered content creation tools can generate quizzes, flashcards, and summaries based on existing educational materials, saving educators time and effort.

AI can also curate personalized learning resources for students, such as articles, videos, and interactive simulations, based on their interests and learning goals. This helps to ensure that students have access to relevant and engaging content that supports their learning.

3. Gamification and Immersive Learning Experiences

AI is enabling the development of gamified and immersive learning experiences that make learning more engaging and interactive. For example, AI-powered educational games can adapt to students' skill levels, providing challenges that are appropriately difficult and rewarding progress with points, badges, and other incentives.

Virtual reality (VR) and augmented reality (AR) technologies, powered by AI, are also being used to create immersive learning experiences. For instance, learners can utilize VR to visit historical landmarks, perform virtual scientific experiments, or hone their abilities in a simulated setting. These immersive experiences can enhance students' understanding and retention of complex concepts.

Challenges in Implementing AI in Education

While AI has the potential to transform education, there are several challenges that must be addressed to ensure its successful implementation. These challenges include technical, ethical, and organizational issues.

1. Data Privacy and Security

The use of AI in education requires the collection and analysis of large amounts of data, including sensitive information about students' performance, behavior, and personal characteristics. This raises significant concerns about data privacy and security, particularly in light of regulations such as the General Data Protection Regulation (GDPR) in Europe and the Family Educational Rights and Privacy Act (FERPA) in the United States.

Ensuring data privacy and security requires robust data governance frameworks, including policies and procedures for data collection, storage, and access. It also requires transparency in how data is used and shared, as well as mechanisms for obtaining informed consent from students and their families.

2. Equity and Access

The adoption of AI in education has the potential to exacerbate existing inequalities, particularly if access to AI-powered tools and platforms is limited to certain groups of students. For example, students in low-income or rural areas may lack the necessary infrastructure, such as high-speed internet or access to devices, to fully benefit from AI-powered education.

Ensuring equity and access requires investment in infrastructure and resources to support all students, regardless of their socioeconomic background. It also requires the development of AI-powered tools and platforms that are accessible to students with disabilities and those who speak different languages.

3. Teacher Training and Support

The successful implementation of AI in education depends on the ability of educators to effectively use AI-powered tools and platforms. This requires ongoing training and support to help educators understand how to integrate AI into their teaching practices and how to interpret and act on the insights provided by AI systems.

Teacher training should also address ethical considerations, such as how to ensure that AI is used in a fair and equitable manner and how to protect students' privacy and data security. Providing educators with the necessary training and support is essential for building trust and confidence in AI-powered education.

4. Bias and Fairness

The performance of AI algorithms is directly tied to the quality of the data used for training, and biased data can result in skewed or unfair results. In education, this can result in AI systems that reinforce existing inequalities or provide unfair advantages to certain groups of students.

Addressing bias and fairness in AI requires careful attention to the data used to train AI algorithms, as well as ongoing monitoring and evaluation to ensure that AI systems are producing fair and equitable outcomes. It also requires the development of ethical guidelines and standards for the use of AI in education.

The Future of AI-Driven Education

The future of AI-driven education is bright, with the potential to transform how we learn and teach. As AI technologies continue to advance, we can expect to see even more innovative applications in education, as well as new opportunities to address some of the most pressing challenges in the field.

1. Lifelong Learning and Skill Development

AI has the potential to support lifelong learning and skill development, enabling individuals to continually update their knowledge and skills throughout their lives. AI-powered learning platforms can provide personalized recommendations for courses, resources, and learning pathways based on individuals' career goals and interests.

For example, AI can help professionals identify skills gaps and recommend training programs to help them stay competitive in the job market. This is especially crucial in a fast-evolving world where new technologies and industries are continually arising.

2. Global Collaboration and Knowledge Sharing

AI can facilitate global collaboration and knowledge sharing, enabling students and educators from around the world to connect and learn from each other. AI-powered translation tools can break down language barriers, making it easier for students to access educational content and participate in online courses and discussions.

AI can also support the development of global learning communities, where students and educators can share resources, collaborate on projects, and learn from diverse perspectives. This can help to foster a more inclusive and interconnected global education system.

3. AI as a Teaching Assistant

In the future, AI could serve as a teaching assistant, helping educators to manage their workload and provide more personalized support to students. For example, AI-powered teaching assistants could grade assignments, provide feedback, and answer students' questions, freeing up educators to focus on more complex and creative aspects of teaching. AI teaching assistants could also provide real-time support during lessons, offering suggestions for how to explain difficult concepts or adapt the lesson to meet the needs of different students. This could help to create a more dynamic and responsive learning environment.

4. Ethical AI and Responsible Innovation

As AI becomes more integrated into education, it will be essential to ensure that it is developed and used in an ethical and responsible manner. This will require ongoing collaboration between stakeholders to develop ethical guidelines, regulatory frameworks, and best practices for AI in education.

It will also be important to engage with students, educators, and the public to ensure that AI technologies are aligned with societal values and priorities. By prioritizing ethical considerations and responsible innovation, we can ensure that AI-driven education benefits all learners and contributes to a more equitable and inclusive society.

In conclusion, AI is transforming education, offering new opportunities to enhance learning and skill development. From personalized learning systems to adaptive learning platforms, AI is enabling more effective, engaging, and accessible education. However, realizing the full potential of AI in education will require addressing challenges related to data privacy, equity, teacher training, and bias. By investing in research and development, fostering collaboration between stakeholders, and ensuring that AI is developed and used in an ethical and responsible manner, we can unlock the transformative the possibilities of AI in education and pave the way for a more promising future for students globally.

3. AI in Cybersecurity: Defending Against Evolving Threats

With the ongoing growth of the digital realm, the number of threats aimed at it also rises. Cybersecurity has become a critical concern for individuals, businesses, and governments alike, as cyberattacks grow in sophistication, frequency, and scale. Traditional cybersecurity measures, while effective to some extent, are often reactive and struggle to keep pace with the rapidly evolving threat landscape. Enter Artificial Intelligence (AI)—a transformative technology that is revolutionizing the field of cybersecurity. By leveraging AI, organizations can proactively detect, respond to, and mitigate cyber threats in real-time, ensuring robust defense mechanisms against increasingly complex attacks. This chapter explores How Artificial Intelligence is Utilized for Identifying and Addressing Threats., its applications in network security and fraud prevention, the challenges in AI-driven cybersecurity, and the future of AI in this critical domain.

How Artificial Intelligence is Utilized for Identifying and Addressing Threats.

AI is playing a pivotal role in enhancing threat detection and response capabilities, enabling organizations to identify and neutralize cyber threats more effectively than ever before. Conventional cybersecurity systems depend on preset rules and known threat signatures to identify risks, making them vulnerable to sophisticated attacks that can evade detection. AI, on the other hand, uses machine learning (ML) and deep learning (DL) algorithms to analyze vast amounts of data, identify patterns, and detect anomalies that may indicate a potential threat.

1. Anomaly Detection

A key use of AI in cybersecurity is identifying unusual patterns. AI tools can examine network traffic, user actions, and system records to determine what constitutes normal behavior. Any activity that strays from this norm is marked as a possible security risk. For example, if an employee's account suddenly starts accessing sensitive files at unusual hours, an AI-powered system can detect this anomaly and alert security teams.

AI-driven anomaly detection is particularly effective in identifying zero-day attacks—previously unknown vulnerabilities that exploit systems before patches are available. By continuously learning and adapting to new data, AI systems can detect unusual patterns that may indicate a zero-day attack, even if the specific threat has never been encountered before.

2. Behavioral Analysis

AI can also be used to analyze user behavior and identify potential insider threats. Insider threats, whether malicious or accidental, are among the most challenging to detect because they originate from within the organization. AI systems can monitor user activity, such as login times, file access patterns, and email communications, to identify behavior that deviates from the norm.

For example, if an employee who typically accesses a limited set of files suddenly starts downloading large volumes of sensitive data, an AI system can flag this activity for further investigation. Behavioral analysis can also help identify compromised accounts, where an attacker has gained unauthorized access to a user's credentials.

3. Automated Threat Response

AI is not only capable of detecting threats but also responding to them in real-time. Automated threat response systems can take immediate action to neutralize a threat, such as isolating an infected device, blocking malicious IP addresses, or terminating suspicious processes. This reduces the time between detection and response, minimizing the potential damage caused by a cyberattack.

For example, AI-powered endpoint detection and response (EDR) solutions can monitor endpoints (such as laptops, smartphones, and servers) for signs of compromise and automatically take action to contain the threat. This is particularly valuable in large organizations with thousands of endpoints, where manual response would be impractical.

4. Threat Intelligence and Predictive Analytics

AI can enhance threat intelligence by analyzing vast amounts of data from multiple sources, including threat feeds, dark web forums, and social media, to identify emerging threats and trends. Predictive analytics can then be used to anticipate future attacks and proactively strengthen defenses.

For example, AI systems can analyze historical attack data to identify patterns and predict the likelihood of specific types of attacks, such as ransomware or phishing campaigns. This enables organizations to prioritize their security efforts and allocate resources more effectively.

Applications of AI in Network Security and Fraud Prevention

AI is also being used to enhance network security and prevent fraud, two critical areas of cybersecurity that are increasingly targeted by cybercriminals.

1. Network Security

AI-powered network security solutions can monitor network traffic in real-time, identifying and blocking malicious activity before it can cause harm. These solutions use machine learning algorithms to analyze network behavior and detect anomalies, such as unusual data transfers or unauthorized access attempts.

For example, AI can be used to detect Distributed Denial of Service (DDoS) attacks, where an attacker overwhelms a network with traffic to disrupt services. AI systems can identify the patterns associated with DDoS attacks and automatically reroute traffic or block malicious IP addresses to mitigate the impact.

AI can also be used to enhance intrusion detection and prevention systems (IDPS). Traditional IDPS rely on signature-based detection, which can be easily bypassed by advanced attacks. AI-powered IDPS, on the other hand, use behavioral analysis to detect anomalies and identify potential intrusions, even if they do not match known attack signatures.

2. Fraud Prevention

AI is playing a crucial role in fraud prevention, particularly in the financial sector. AI-powered fraud detection systems can analyze transaction data in real-time, identifying patterns and anomalies that may indicate fraudulent activity.

For example, AI can be used to detect credit card fraud by analyzing transaction data and identifying unusual spending patterns, such as large purchases in a foreign country or multiple transactions in a short period. AI systems can also analyze user behavior, such as login locations and device usage, to identify potential account takeovers.

In addition to detecting fraud, AI can also be used to prevent it. For example, AI-powered authentication systems can use biometric data, such as facial recognition or fingerprint scanning, to verify user identity and prevent unauthorized access.

3. Phishing and Social Engineering Detection

Phishing and social engineering attacks are among the most common and effective methods used by cybercriminals to gain unauthorized access to systems and data. AI can be used to detect and prevent these attacks by analyzing email content, URLs, and user behavior.

For example, AI-powered email security solutions can analyze the content of incoming emails to identify phishing attempts, such as suspicious links or attachments. AI can also analyze the behavior of users who interact with phishing emails, such as clicking on links or entering credentials, to identify potential compromises.

Challenges in AI-Driven Cybersecurity

While AI offers significant advantages in cybersecurity, it also presents several challenges that must be addressed to ensure its effective and ethical use.

1. Data Privacy and Security

The use of AI in cybersecurity requires the collection and analysis of large amounts of data, including sensitive information such as user behavior, network traffic, and transaction data. This raises significant concerns about data privacy and security, particularly in light of regulations such as the General Data Protection Regulation (GDPR) and the California Consumer Privacy Act (CCPA).

Ensuring data privacy and security requires robust data governance frameworks, including policies and procedures for data collection, storage, and access. It also requires transparency in how data is used and shared, as well as mechanisms for obtaining informed consent from users.

2. Bias and Fairness

The performance of AI algorithms is directly tied to the quality of the data used for training, and biased data can result in skewed or unfair results. In cybersecurity, this can result in AI systems that unfairly target certain groups or fail to detect threats in specific contexts.

For example, an AI-powered fraud detection system that is trained on data from a specific demographic may not perform well for other demographics, leading to false positives or false negatives. Addressing bias and fairness in AI requires careful attention to the data used to train algorithms, as well as ongoing monitoring and evaluation to ensure that AI systems are producing fair and equitable outcomes.

3. Adversarial Attacks

AI systems themselves can be targeted by cybercriminals through adversarial attacks, where attackers manipulate input data to deceive AI algorithms. For example, an attacker could modify a malicious file to evade detection by an AI-powered antivirus system or use adversarial examples to bypass facial recognition systems.

Defending against adversarial attacks requires the development of robust AI models that are resistant to manipulation, as well as ongoing research into new defense mechanisms. It also requires collaboration between cybersecurity experts and AI researchers to identify and mitigate potential vulnerabilities.

4. Skill Gaps and Resource Constraints

Successfully integrating AI into cybersecurity demands specific expertise and resources, which many organizations may not possess. Developing and deploying AI-powered cybersecurity solutions requires expertise in machine learning, data science, and cybersecurity, as well as access to high-quality data and computational resources.

Addressing skill gaps and resource constraints requires investment in training and education, as well as collaboration between industry, academia, and government to develop the necessary talent and infrastructure.

The Future of AI in Cybersecurity

The future of AI in cybersecurity is promising, with the potential to transform how organizations defend against evolving threats. As AI technologies continue to advance, we can expect to see even more innovative applications in cybersecurity, as well as new opportunities to address some of the most pressing challenges in the field.

1. Autonomous Cybersecurity Systems

In the future, AI-powered cybersecurity systems may become fully autonomous, capable of detecting, responding to, and mitigating threats without human intervention. These systems would use advanced machine learning algorithms to continuously learn and adapt to new threats, providing real-time protection against even the most sophisticated attacks.

Autonomous cybersecurity systems could also be used to manage and secure large-scale networks, such as those used in critical infrastructure or smart cities. By handling repetitive security tasks automatically, these systems allow human experts to concentrate on more intricate and high-level issues.

2. AI-Driven Threat Hunting

AI can improve threat detection by automating the identification and examination of possible security risks. AI-powered threat hunting tools can analyze vast amounts of data from multiple sources, such as network logs, endpoint data, and threat intelligence feeds, to identify patterns and anomalies that may indicate a potential threat.

These tools can also provide recommendations for further investigation, helping security analysts to prioritize their efforts and respond more effectively to emerging threats. AI-driven threat hunting can help organizations stay ahead of cybercriminals by identifying and neutralizing threats before they can cause harm.

3. Collaborative AI Ecosystems

The future of AI in cybersecurity may also involve the development of collaborative AI ecosystems, where multiple organizations share threat intelligence and collaborate on defense strategies. AI-powered platforms could enable organizations to share data on emerging threats, attack patterns, and defense mechanisms, creating a collective defense against cyber threats.

Collaborative AI ecosystems could also be used to develop and deploy shared security solutions, such as AI-powered threat detection and response systems, that benefit all participants. This would help to level the playing field for smaller organizations that may lack the resources to develop their own AI-powered cybersecurity solutions.

4. Ethical AI and Responsible Innovation

As AI becomes more integrated into cybersecurity, it will be essential to ensure that it is developed and used in an ethical and responsible manner. This will require ongoing collaboration between stakeholders to develop ethical guidelines, regulatory frameworks, and best practices for AI in cybersecurity.

It will also be important to engage with users, organizations, and the public to ensure that AI technologies are aligned with societal values and priorities. By prioritizing ethical considerations and responsible innovation, we can ensure that AI-driven cybersecurity benefits all stakeholders and contributes to a safer and more secure digital world.

In conclusion, AI is transforming cybersecurity, offering new opportunities to defend against evolving threats. From threat detection and response to network security and fraud prevention, AI is enabling more effective, proactive, and adaptive cybersecurity solutions. However, realizing the full potential of AI in cybersecurity will require addressing challenges related to data privacy, bias, adversarial attacks, and skill gaps. By investing in research and development, fostering collaboration between stakeholders, and ensuring that AI is developed and used in an ethical and responsible manner, we can unlock the transformative potential of AI in cybersecurity and create a safer digital future for all.

4. AI in Finance: Revolutionizing Banking, Investing, and Risk Management

The financial industry is undergoing a profound transformation, driven by the rapid adoption of Artificial Intelligence (AI). From banking and investing to risk management and fraud detection, AI is revolutionizing how financial institutions operate, making processes more efficient, accurate, and customer-centric. By leveraging machine learning (ML), natural language processing (NLP), and predictive analytics, AI is enabling financial institutions to analyze vast amounts of data, uncover insights, and make data-driven decisions in real-time. This chapter explores the applications of AI in fraud detection, algorithmic trading, and credit scoring, the challenges in AI-driven financial systems, and the future of AI in finance.

Applications of AI in Fraud Detection, Algorithmic Trading, and Credit Scoring

AI is being applied across a wide range of financial services, transforming traditional processes and enabling new capabilities. Below, we delve into three key areas where AI is making a significant impact: fraud detection, algorithmic trading, and credit scoring.

1. Fraud Detection

Fraud is a persistent and evolving challenge for financial institutions, costing billions of dollars annually. Traditional fraud detection systems rely on rule-based approaches, which are often reactive and struggle to keep pace with increasingly sophisticated fraud schemes. AI, on the other hand, offers a proactive and adaptive solution to fraud detection.

a. Instant Transaction Oversight

AI-driven tools can evaluate transaction information instantly, identifying trends and irregularities that could point to potential fraud. For instance, if a credit card is used for a significant purchase abroad shortly after a minor transaction in the cardholder's home country, the AI system can flag this as suspicious and prompt additional verification steps.

Machine learning models can enhance their precision by training on past fraud data, becoming more effective as they learn. By continuously updating their models based on new data, AI systems can adapt to emerging fraud trends and detect previously unknown fraud schemes.

b. Behavioral Biometrics

AI is also being used to enhance fraud detection through behavioral biometrics, which analyze user behavior to verify identity. For example, AI systems can monitor how a user interacts with a mobile banking app, including typing speed, swipe patterns, and device orientation. If the behavior deviates from the user's normal patterns, the system can flag the activity as potentially fraudulent.

Behavioral biometrics provide an additional layer of security, particularly for online and mobile banking, where traditional authentication methods, such as passwords and PINs, may be vulnerable to theft or phishing attacks.

c. Phishing and Social Engineering Detection

AI can also be used to detect and prevent phishing and social engineering attacks, which are often used to steal sensitive financial information. AI-powered email security solutions can analyze the content of incoming emails to identify phishing attempts, such as suspicious links or attachments. Similarly, AI can analyze social media activity to detect potential social engineering attacks, such as fake profiles or fraudulent messages.

2. Algorithmic Trading

Algorithmic trading, also known as algo-trading, involves the use of computer algorithms to execute trades at high speeds and volumes. AI is taking algorithmic trading to the next level by enabling more sophisticated and adaptive trading strategies.

a. Predictive Analytics

AI-powered predictive analytics can analyze vast amounts of financial data, including market trends, news articles, and social media sentiment, to predict price movements and identify trading opportunities. For example, AI systems can analyze historical price data to identify patterns that may indicate an upcoming price increase or decrease.

Predictive analytics can also be used to forecast market volatility, enabling traders to adjust their strategies in real-time. This is particularly valuable in fast-moving markets, where even small delays in decision-making can result in significant losses.

b. Sentiment Analysis

AI can analyze news articles, social media posts, and other textual data to gauge market sentiment and predict its impact on asset prices. For example, if a company announces positive earnings results, an AI system can analyze the sentiment of news articles and social media posts to predict how the market will react.

Sentiment analysis can also be used to identify emerging trends and themes in the market, enabling traders to capitalize on new opportunities before they become widely recognized.

c. High-Frequency Trading

AI is also being used in high-frequency trading (HFT), where algorithms execute trades in milliseconds to take advantage of small price discrepancies. AI-driven high-frequency trading (HFT) systems can process market information instantly, spot arbitrage possibilities, and carry out transactions at incredible speeds.

HFT is particularly valuable in highly liquid markets, where even small price movements can result in significant profits. However, it also requires sophisticated risk management systems to prevent losses due to market volatility or technical glitches.

3. Credit Scoring

Credit scoring is a critical component of the lending process, enabling financial institutions to assess the creditworthiness of borrowers. Traditional credit scoring models rely on a limited set of factors, such as credit history and income, which may not provide a complete picture of a borrower's financial situation. AI is transforming credit scoring by enabling more comprehensive and accurate assessments.

a. Alternative Data Sources

AI-powered credit scoring models can analyze alternative data sources, such as utility payments, rental history, and even social media activity, to assess creditworthiness. This is particularly valuable for individuals with limited credit history, such as young adults or recent immigrants, who may be underserved by traditional credit scoring models.

By incorporating alternative data sources, AI-powered credit scoring models can provide a more accurate and inclusive assessment of credit risk, enabling financial institutions to extend credit to a broader range of borrowers.

b. Dynamic Credit Scoring

AI can also enable dynamic credit scoring, where credit scores are updated in real-time based on changes in a borrower's financial situation. For example, if a borrower pays off a large debt or experiences a significant increase in income, an AI-powered credit scoring system can update their credit score accordingly.

Dynamic credit scoring provides a more accurate and up-to-date assessment of credit risk, enabling financial institutions to make more informed lending decisions. It also provides borrowers with greater transparency and control over their credit scores, as they can see how their financial behavior impacts their creditworthiness in real-time.

c. Risk-Based Pricing

AI-powered credit scoring models can also enable risk-based pricing, where the interest rate on a loan is adjusted based on the borrower's credit risk. For example, a borrower with a high credit score may receive a lower interest rate, while a borrower with a lower credit score may receive a higher interest rate.

Risk-based pricing enables financial institutions to offer more competitive loan products, while also managing their risk exposure. It also provides borrowers with greater flexibility and choice, as they can select loan products that align with their financial situation and risk tolerance.

Challenges in AI-Driven Financial Systems

While AI offers significant advantages in finance, it also presents several challenges that must be addressed to ensure its effective and ethical use.

1. Data Privacy and Security

Implementing AI in finance involves gathering and examining vast quantities of sensitive data, such as personal and financial details. This raises significant concerns about data privacy and security, particularly in light of regulations such as the General Data Protection Regulation (GDPR) and the California Consumer Privacy Act (CCPA).

Ensuring data privacy and security requires robust data governance frameworks, including policies and procedures for data collection, storage, and access. It also requires transparency in how data is used and shared, as well as mechanisms for obtaining informed consent from users.

2. Bias and Fairness

The performance of AI algorithms is directly tied to the quality of the data used for training, and biased data can result in skewed or unfair results. In finance, this can result in AI systems that unfairly discriminate against certain groups or fail to accurately assess credit risk.

For example, an AI-powered credit scoring model that is trained on data from a specific demographic may not perform well for other demographics, leading to unfair lending practices. Addressing bias and fairness in AI requires careful attention to the data used to train algorithms, as well as ongoing monitoring and evaluation to ensure that AI systems are producing fair and equitable outcomes.

3. Regulatory Compliance

The use of AI in finance is subject to a complex and evolving regulatory landscape, which can vary significantly across different jurisdictions. Financial institutions must ensure that their AI systems comply with relevant regulations, such as anti-money laundering (AML) laws, know-your-customer (KYC) requirements, and consumer protection laws.

Ensuring regulatory compliance requires ongoing monitoring and evaluation of AI systems, as well as collaboration with regulators to develop and implement best practices for AI in finance.

4. Explainability and Transparency

AI systems, particularly those based on deep learning, often operate as "black boxes," meaning that their decision-making processes are not easily understood by humans. This lack of transparency can make it difficult to assess whether an AI system is making fair and accurate decisions, and it can also make it challenging to hold AI systems accountable for their actions.

Ensuring explainability and transparency in AI requires the development of interpretable AI models, as well as mechanisms for providing clear and understandable explanations for AI-driven decisions. This is particularly important in high-stakes applications, such as credit scoring and fraud detection, where AI decisions can have significant impacts on individuals' lives.

The Future of AI in Finance

The future of AI in finance is bright, with the potential to transform how financial institutions operate and interact with their customers. As AI technologies continue to advance, we can expect to see even more innovative applications in finance, as well as new opportunities to address some of the most pressing challenges in the field.

1. Personalized Financial Services

AI has the potential to enable highly personalized financial services, tailored to the individual needs and preferences of each customer. For example, AI-powered financial advisors can provide personalized investment recommendations based on a customer's financial goals, risk tolerance, and market conditions.

Similarly, AI-powered budgeting tools can analyze a customer's spending patterns and provide personalized recommendations for saving and investing. This level of personalization can help customers achieve their financial goals more effectively and build stronger relationships with their financial institutions.

2. Enhanced Risk Management

AI can enhance risk management by enabling more accurate and comprehensive assessments of risk. For example, AI-powered risk models can analyze a wide range of data sources, including market trends, economic indicators, and geopolitical events, to predict potential risks and their impact on financial markets.

AI can also enable real-time risk monitoring, where financial institutions can continuously assess their risk exposure and adjust their strategies accordingly. This is particularly valuable in fast-moving markets, where even small changes in risk can have significant impacts on financial performance.

3. AI-Driven Financial Inclusion

AI has the potential to promote financial inclusion by enabling more accurate and inclusive assessments of creditworthiness. By incorporating alternative data sources and dynamic credit scoring, AI-powered credit scoring models can extend credit to underserved populations, such as individuals with limited credit history or those in developing countries.

AI can also enable the development of innovative financial products and services, such as microfinance and peer-to-peer lending, that are tailored to the needs of underserved populations. This can help to bridge the gap between traditional financial services and the unbanked or underbanked populations.

4. Ethical AI and Responsible Innovation

As AI becomes more integrated into finance, it will be essential to ensure that it is developed and used in an ethical and responsible manner. This will require ongoing collaboration between stakeholders to develop ethical guidelines, regulatory frameworks, and best practices for AI in finance.

It will also be important to engage with customers, regulators, and the public to ensure that AI technologies are aligned with societal values and priorities. By prioritizing ethical considerations and responsible innovation, we can ensure that AI-driven finance benefits all stakeholders and contributes to a more equitable and inclusive financial system.

In conclusion, AI is revolutionizing finance, offering new opportunities to enhance efficiency, accuracy, and customer-centricity. From fraud detection and algorithmic trading to credit scoring and risk management, AI is enabling financial institutions to make data-driven decisions and deliver personalized services. However, realizing the full potential of AI in finance will require addressing challenges related to data privacy, bias, regulatory compliance, and explainability. By investing in research and development, fostering collaboration between stakeholders, and ensuring that AI is developed and used in an ethical and responsible manner, we can unlock the transformative potential of AI in finance and create a brighter future for the financial industry.

Dear Reader,

Thank you for joining me on this journey through **AI Trends in 2025!** I hope you're finding the book as engaging and meaningful as I intended it to be. Your thoughts and feedback mean a great deal to me.

If you've enjoyed the book so far, sharing your honest review on Amazon can help other readers discover it. Reviews are incredibly valuable, not only to authors like me but also to those searching for their next read.

Whether it's a quick note about what resonated with you or a detailed reflection, your feedback is always appreciated.

Book   link:
https://www.amazon.com/dp/B0DRTK49ZN

Thank you for your time, support, and for being a part of this story.

Section 5: The Future of AI

1. Artificial General Intelligence (AGI)

Hypothetical AI Systems Capable of Human-Level Reasoning and Adaptability Across Diverse Tasks

Introduction

Artificial General Intelligence (AGI) represents the pinnacle of artificial intelligence research—a hypothetical system capable of performing any intellectual task that a human can do. Unlike Narrow AI, which is designed for specific tasks (e.g., image recognition, language translation, or playing chess), AGI would possess the ability to reason, learn, and adapt across a wide range of domains, much like a human. This level of intelligence would enable AGI to solve complex problems, innovate, and even exhibit creativity, making it a transformative force in science, technology, and society.

The idea of Artificial General Intelligence (AGI) has captivated scientists, thinkers, and futurists for many years. While Narrow AI has made remarkable progress in recent years, AGI remains an elusive goal. Achieving AGI would require breakthroughs in areas such as cognitive architecture, learning algorithms, and understanding the nature of intelligence itself. As we move closer to this goal, it is essential to explore the principles, challenges, and implications of AGI to ensure that its development is guided by ethical considerations and aligned with human values.

This part explores the idea of AGI, its development, possible uses, obstacles, and the future prospects of this transformative technology.

What is Artificial General Intelligence (AGI)?

Artificial General Intelligence (AGI) describes AI systems capable of comprehending, learning, and utilizing knowledge across diverse tasks with a proficiency similar to that of human intelligence.. Unlike Narrow AI, which is specialized for specific tasks, AGI would exhibit flexibility, adaptability, and generalization, enabling it to perform any intellectual task that a human can do.

Key Characteristics of AGI

1. Generalization: AGI can apply knowledge learned in one domain to solve problems in entirely different domains.

2. Adaptability: AGI can adapt to new situations and learn from experience, much like humans.

3. Reasoning and Problem-Solving: AGI can reason abstractly, solve complex problems, and make decisions based on incomplete or ambiguous information.

4. Creativity: AGI can generate novel ideas, solutions, and artistic expressions.

5. Self-Awareness: Some definitions of AGI include self-awareness, or the ability to understand and reflect on one's own existence and thought processes.

Why AGI Matters

-   Unprecedented Capabilities: AGI could revolutionize fields such as science, medicine, engineering, and art by solving problems that are currently beyond human capabilities.
-   Economic and Social Impact: AGI could transform industries, create new opportunities, and address global challenges such as climate change, poverty, and disease.
-   Ethical and Philosophical Questions: The development of AGI raises profound questions about the nature

of intelligence, consciousness, and the relationship between humans and machines.

The Evolution of AGI

The idea of Artificial General Intelligence (AGI) originates from the initial stages of artificial intelligence research. Early innovators like Alan Turing and John McCarthy imagined machines capable of human-like thought and reasoning. Over the years, advancements in computing capabilities, algorithms, and access to data have fueled the growth of AI. Yet, achieving AGI is still a far-off objective, with substantial technical and philosophical hurdles yet to be addressed.

Key Milestones in AGI Research

1. Early Visionaries: Alan Turing's seminal paper "Computing Machinery and Intelligence" (1950) introduced the idea of machines that could exhibit intelligent behavior. In 1956, John McCarthy introduced the term "Artificial Intelligence" and established the foundational principles for AGI research.

2. Cognitive Architectures: Researchers such as Marvin Minsky and Allen Newell developed early cognitive architectures, such as the Society of Mind and SOAR, which aimed to model human reasoning and problem-solving.

3. Machine Learning Revolution: The rise of machine learning, particularly deep learning, has enabled

significant progress in Narrow AI. However, these approaches are limited in their ability to generalize across tasks.

4. Neuroscience and AI: Advances in neuroscience have provided insights into the workings of the human brain, inspiring new approaches to AGI, such as neural-symbolic systems and brain-inspired architectures.

5. Ethical and Philosophical Discussions: The potential implications of AGI have sparked debates about its ethical development, safety, and societal impact.

The Future of AGI (2025 and Beyond)

By 2025, AGI research is expected to focus on several key areas:

- Cognitive Architectures: Developing unified frameworks that integrate perception, reasoning, learning, and memory.

- Transfer Learning: Enabling AI systems to transfer knowledge across domains and tasks.

- Neurosymbolic AI: Integrating the capabilities of neural networks with symbolic reasoning to attain intelligence that more closely resembles human cognition.

- Ethical and Secure AGI: Guaranteeing that AGI systems align with human values and remain controllable and comprehensible to humans.

Potential Applications of AGI

The development of AGI would have far-reaching implications across industries and domains. Below are some of the key areas where AGI could make a transformative impact:

1. Science and Research

- Drug Discovery: AGI could accelerate the discovery of new drugs by analyzing complex biological data and simulating molecular interactions.
- Climate Modeling: AGI could develop more accurate climate models and propose innovative solutions to mitigate climate change.
- Space Exploration: AGI could autonomously conduct scientific experiments, analyze data, and make

decisions in space exploration missions.

2. Healthcare

- Personalized Medicine: AGI could analyze patient data to develop personalized treatment plans tailored to individual genetic profiles and medical histories.
- Medical Diagnosis: AGI could diagnose diseases with high accuracy by integrating data from medical imaging, lab tests, and patient records.
- Surgical Assistance: AGI could assist surgeons in complex procedures by providing real-time guidance and decision support.

3. Education

- Personalized Learning: AGI could create customized learning experiences for students, adapting to their individual needs and learning styles.
- Tutoring and Mentoring: AGI could serve as a tutor or mentor, providing personalized feedback and guidance to learners.
- Curriculum Design: AGI could design and optimize educational curricula based on the latest research and student performance data.

4. Business and Industry

- Strategic Planning: AGI could analyze market trends, competitor strategies, and internal data to develop optimal business strategies.

- Supply Chain Optimization: AGI could optimize supply chain operations by predicting demand, managing inventory, and coordinating logistics.
- Innovation and R&D: AGI could drive innovation by generating new ideas, designing products, and solving complex engineering problems.

5. Creative Arts

- Art and Music: AGI could create original works of art, music, and literature, pushing the boundaries of creativity.
- Film and Media: AGI could assist in scriptwriting, animation, and special effects, enhancing the production of films and media content.

- Design: AGI could design buildings, products, and user interfaces, combining functionality with aesthetic appeal.

6. Social and Global Challenges

- Poverty Alleviation: AGI could analyze socioeconomic data to develop strategies for reducing poverty and inequality.
- Disaster Response: AGI could coordinate disaster response efforts by analyzing real-time data and optimizing resource allocation.
- Public Policy: AGI could assist policymakers by analyzing complex data and simulating the impact of policy decisions.

Challenges in Developing AGI

Despite its potential, the development of AGI faces several significant challenges that must be addressed to ensure its successful realization.

1. Technical Challenges

- Cognitive Architecture: Developing a unified cognitive architecture that integrates perception, reasoning, learning, and memory is a complex task.
- Generalization: Achieving the ability to generalize knowledge across diverse domains remains a major hurdle.
- Learning Efficiency: AGI systems must be able to learn efficiently from limited data, much like humans.

2. Ethical and Safety Challenges

- Alignment: Ensuring that AGI systems are aligned with human values and ethical principles is critical to preventing unintended consequences.
- Control: Developing mechanisms to control and regulate AGI systems is essential to ensuring their safe and responsible use.
- Bias and Fairness: AGI systems must be designed to avoid biases and ensure fairness in decision-making.

3. Philosophical Challenges

- Consciousness: The nature of consciousness and whether AGI systems could achieve self-awareness remains a topic of debate.

- Moral Status: The moral status of AGI systems and their rights and responsibilities raise profound ethical questions.
- Existential Risks: The potential risks posed by AGI, including the possibility of superintelligent systems, require careful consideration and mitigation.

4. Societal Challenges

- Economic Impact: The widespread adoption of AGI could disrupt labor markets and economies, requiring new approaches to education, employment, and social welfare.
- Regulation: Developing regulatory frameworks to govern the development and use of AGI is

essential to ensuring its responsible deployment.

- Public Acceptance: Building public trust and acceptance of AGI will require transparent communication and engagement with stakeholders.

The Future of AGI

The prospects for AGI are filled with both promise and unpredictability. While significant technical and ethical challenges remain, the potential benefits of AGI are immense. By 2025 and beyond, AGI research is expected to focus on several key areas:

Key Trends

- Cognitive Architectures: Developing unified frameworks that integrate perception, reasoning, learning, and memory.

- Transfer Learning: Enabling AI systems to transfer knowledge across domains and tasks.

- Neurosymbolic AI: Integrating the capabilities of neural networks with symbolic reasoning to attain intelligence that more closely resembles human cognition.

- Ethical and Secure AGI: Guaranteeing that AGI systems align with human values and remain controllable and comprehensible to humans.

Conclusion

Artificial General Intelligence (AGI) represents the ultimate goal of AI research—a system capable of human-level reasoning and adaptability across diverse tasks. While AGI remains a hypothetical concept, its potential to transform industries, solve complex problems, and address global challenges is unparalleled. However, the development of AGI also raises profound ethical, philosophical, and societal questions that must be addressed to ensure its responsible and beneficial use. As we move closer to the realization of AGI, it is essential to approach its development with caution, transparency, and a commitment to ethical principles. By fostering collaboration between researchers, policymakers, and stakeholders, we can unlock the full potential of AGI and create a future where AI serves as a force for good, benefiting all of humanity.

2. AI and the Future of Work: Reshaping Jobs and Industries

Artificial Intelligence (AI) has moved beyond being a futuristic idea limited to science fiction. It is a present-day reality that is rapidly transforming the way we live, work, and interact with the world around us. As AI technologies continue to evolve, they are reshaping industries, redefining job roles, and creating new opportunities while simultaneously posing challenges that society must address. The future of work in an AI-dominated world is a topic of immense importance, as it touches on economic, social, and ethical dimensions. This essay explores how AI is transforming the workforce, the implications of AI-driven automation on job displacement, the need for upskilling and reskilling, and what the future of work might look like in an AI-dominated world.

How AI is Transforming the Workforce

AI is revolutionizing the workforce by augmenting human capabilities, automating repetitive tasks, and enabling new forms of productivity. From healthcare to manufacturing, finance to retail, AI is being integrated into various industries, driving efficiency, innovation, and growth. Below are some key ways in which AI is transforming the workforce:

1. Augmenting Human Capabilities

AI is not just about replacing human labor; it is also about enhancing human capabilities. Tools like machine learning algorithms, natural language processing (NLP), and computer vision are enabling workers to perform tasks more efficiently and accurately. For example, in healthcare, AI-powered diagnostic tools assist doctors in identifying diseases with greater precision. In creative industries, AI tools like ChatGPT and DALL·E are helping writers, designers, and artists generate ideas and content faster.

2. Automating Repetitive Tasks

One of the most significant impacts of AI on the workforce is its ability to automate repetitive and mundane tasks. In industries like manufacturing, logistics, and customer service, AI-driven robots and software are taking over tasks such as assembly line work, inventory management, and responding to customer inquiries. This automation allows human workers to focus on more complex, creative, and strategic tasks.

3. Enabling Data-Driven Decision-Making

AI excels at analyzing vast amounts of data and extracting actionable insights. In sectors like finance, marketing, and supply chain management, AI-powered analytics tools are helping businesses make data-driven decisions. For instance, AI algorithms can predict market trends, optimize pricing strategies, and identify potential risks, enabling companies to stay competitive in a fast-paced economy.

4. *Creating New Job Roles*

While AI is automating certain tasks, it is also creating new job roles that did not exist before. Roles such as AI ethicists, machine learning engineers, data scientists, and AI trainers are in great demand. These positions require specialized skills and knowledge, highlighting the need for continuous learning and adaptation in the workforce.

5. *Enhancing Remote Work and Collaboration*

The COVID-19 pandemic accelerated the adoption of remote work, and AI is playing a crucial role in making remote collaboration more effective. AI-powered tools like virtual assistants, project management software, and video conferencing platforms are helping teams stay connected and productive, regardless of their physical location.

AI-Driven Automation and Job Displacement

Although AI provides many advantages, it also brings up worries about job loss. As AI systems become more capable, there is a growing fear that machines will replace human workers, leading to widespread unemployment and economic inequality. This section examines the impact of AI-driven automation on jobs and the potential consequences for the workforce.

1. The Scale of Automation

AI-driven automation is already affecting jobs across various sectors. A McKinsey report suggests that as many as 800 million jobs globally might be automated by 2030. Jobs that involve routine, repetitive tasks are most at risk, including roles in manufacturing, retail, and administrative support. However, even jobs that require higher levels of skill and expertise, such as legal research and financial analysis, are not immune to automation.

2. Economic and Social Implications

The displacement of jobs due to AI-driven automation has significant economic and social implications. On the one hand, automation can lead to increased productivity and economic growth. On the other hand, it can exacerbate income inequality and create a skills gap, as workers who lose their jobs may struggle to find new employment in an AI-driven economy.

3. The Role of Policymakers

To tackle the issues of job loss, policymakers need to take an active approach.. This includes implementing policies that support workers during transitions, such as unemployment benefits, job placement services, and incentives for businesses to retrain employees. Additionally, governments should invest in education and training programs to equip workers with the skills needed for the jobs of the future.

4. Ethical Considerations

The moral consequences of AI-powered automation must not be ignored. Questions about fairness, accountability, and transparency arise when machines make decisions that affect human lives. For example, if an AI system is used to screen job applicants, how can we ensure that it does not perpetuate biases or discriminate against certain groups?

Tackling these ethical issues is crucial for fostering trust in AI technologies.

Upskilling and Reskilling for an AI-Driven Economy

As AI continues to reshape the workforce, the need for upskilling and reskilling has never been more urgent. Workers must adapt to the changing demands of the labor market by acquiring new skills and knowledge. This section explores the importance of lifelong learning and the strategies that individuals, businesses, and governments can adopt to prepare for an AI-driven economy.

1. The Importance of Lifelong Learning

In an AI-driven economy, the skills that are in demand today may become obsolete tomorrow. Continuous learning is crucial for employees to remain relevant and competitive. This includes not only technical skills, such as programming and data analysis, but also soft skills, such as critical thinking, creativity, and emotional intelligence.

2. *Strategies for Upskilling and Reskilling*

- Individual Responsibility: Workers must take ownership of their career development by seeking out learning opportunities, whether through online courses, certifications, or on-the-job training.
- Corporate Training Programs: Businesses have a vested interest in upskilling their employees. Companies can offer training programs, mentorship opportunities, and incentives for employees to learn new skills.
- Government Initiatives: Governments can support upskilling and reskilling efforts by funding education programs, partnering with industry leaders, and

creating policies that encourage lifelong learning.

3. The Role of Educational Institutions

Educational institutions must adapt their curricula to meet the needs of an AI-driven economy. This includes incorporating AI and data science into traditional disciplines, offering interdisciplinary programs, and providing students with hands-on experience through internships and projects.

4. Addressing the Digital Divide

Access to education and training is not equal across all segments of society. To ensure that everyone can benefit from the opportunities created by AI, it is essential to address the digital divide. This includes providing affordable internet access, digital literacy training, and resources for underserved communities.

The Future of Work in an AI-Dominated World

As AI technologies continue to advance, the future of work will be shaped by a combination of opportunities and challenges. This section explores what the future might look like in an AI-dominated world and how society can navigate this transformation.

1. The Rise of Hybrid Work Models

The future of work is likely to be characterized by hybrid models that combine human and machine capabilities. In this scenario, AI systems handle routine tasks, while humans focus on tasks that require creativity, empathy, and complex decision-making. This collaboration between humans and machines has the potential to drive innovation and productivity to new heights.

2. The Gig Economy and Flexible Work Arrangements

AI is also enabling the growth of the gig economy and flexible work arrangements. Platforms powered by AI algorithms connect workers with short-term jobs and freelance opportunities, offering greater flexibility and autonomy. Yet, this change also brings up worries about job stability, benefits, and employee rights.

3. The Importance of Human-Centric AI

As AI becomes more integrated into the workplace, it is crucial to ensure that it is designed and deployed in a way that prioritizes human well-being. This includes creating AI systems that are transparent, fair, and accountable, as well as fostering a culture of collaboration and trust between humans and machines.

4. The Role of Universal Basic Income (UBI)

Some experts have proposed Universal Basic Income (UBI) as a solution to the potential job displacement caused by AI. UBI would provide all citizens with a regular, unconditional sum of money, ensuring a basic standard of living regardless of employment status. While UBI is a controversial idea, it highlights the need for innovative solutions to address the economic challenges posed by AI.

5. A Global Perspective

The impact of AI on the future of work is not limited to individual countries; it is a global phenomenon. Developing countries, in particular, face unique challenges and opportunities as they navigate the AI revolution. International cooperation and knowledge-sharing will be essential to ensure that the benefits of AI are distributed equitably across the world.

Conclusion

AI is undoubtedly transforming the future of work, presenting both possibilities and difficulties. While AI-driven automation has the potential to increase productivity and create new job roles, it also poses risks such as job displacement and economic inequality. To navigate this transformation, individuals, businesses, and governments must prioritize upskilling and reskilling, adopt ethical AI practices, and foster a culture of lifelong learning.

The future of work in an AI-dominated world will be characterized by hybrid work models, flexible arrangements, and a focus on human-centric AI. By embracing these changes and addressing the associated challenges, society can harness the power of AI to create a more inclusive, innovative, and prosperous future for all. The journey ahead is complex, but with thoughtful planning and collaboration, we can ensure that AI serves as a force for good in the world of work.

3. AI in Robotics: Bridging the Gap Between Physical and Digital Worlds

The integration of Artificial Intelligence (AI) into robotics represents one of the most transformative technological advancements of the 21st century. By combining the computational power of AI with the physical capabilities of robots, we are witnessing the emergence of intelligent machines that can perceive, learn, reason, and interact with their surroundings in ways that were previously only imagined in science fiction. This convergence of AI and robotics is bridging the gap between the physical and digital worlds, enabling robots to perform complex tasks, adapt to dynamic environments, and collaborate with humans in unprecedented ways. This essay explores the role of AI in robotics, its applications across industries, the challenges it presents, and its potential to reshape our world.

The Evolution of AI in Robotics

The domain of robotics has advanced significantly since its beginnings. Early robots were primarily mechanical devices programmed to perform repetitive tasks in controlled environments, such as assembly lines in manufacturing plants. These robots lacked the ability to perceive or adapt to their surroundings, limiting their utility to highly structured settings.

The advent of AI has revolutionized robotics by enabling machines to process sensory data, make decisions, and learn from experience. AI-powered robots are no longer confined to pre-programmed routines; they can now navigate complex environments, interact with humans, and even exhibit a degree of autonomy. This evolution has been driven by advancements in machine learning, computer vision, natural language processing, and sensor technologies.

Key Milestones in AI-Driven Robotics

- Industrial Robots: The first wave of robotics was dominated by industrial robots, which were designed to automate repetitive tasks in manufacturing. These robots were highly efficient but lacked flexibility and adaptability.

- Service Robots: The integration of AI enabled the development of service robots, which are designed to assist humans in various settings, such as healthcare, hospitality, and domestic environments. Examples include robotic vacuum cleaners, delivery robots, and robotic assistants for the elderly.

- Collaborative Robots (Cobots): Cobots are created to operate alongside humans in shared environments. Equipped with AI, these robots can perceive human actions, adapt to changes, and ensure safety through advanced sensors and algorithms.

- Autonomous Robots: The latest generation of robots leverages AI to achieve full autonomy. These robots can operate in unstructured environments, such as disaster zones, underwater, or outer space, without human intervention.

How AI Enhances Robotics

AI serves as the "brain" of modern robots, enabling them to perform tasks that require perception, decision-making, and learning.

Below are some of the key ways in which AI enhances robotics:

1. Perception and Sensing

AI enables robots to perceive their environments through sensors such as cameras, LiDAR, and microphones. Computer vision algorithms allow robots to recognize objects, detect obstacles, and navigate complex spaces. For example, autonomous vehicles use AI to interpret visual data and make real-time driving decisions.

2. Learning and Adaptation

Machine learning algorithms enable robots to learn from data and enhance their capabilities progressively. Reinforcement learning, specifically, allows robots to learn by experimenting, making them more flexible when tackling new tasks and environments. For instance, robotic arms in warehouses can learn to pick and pack items more efficiently by analyzing past performance.

3. Decision-Making and Autonomy

AI empowers robots to make decisions based on sensory input and predefined goals. This capability is crucial for applications such as search and rescue missions, where robots must navigate unpredictable environments and prioritize tasks autonomously.

4. Human-Robot Interaction

Natural language processing (NLP) and speech recognition technologies enable robots to understand and respond to human commands. This capability is essential for service robots, such as customer service bots and robotic companions, which must interact with humans in a natural and intuitive manner.

5. Predictive Maintenance

AI algorithms can analyze data from robotic systems to predict when maintenance is needed, reducing downtime and extending the lifespan of the equipment. This is particularly valuable in industrial settings, where robot failures can disrupt production.

Applications of AI in Robotics

The combination of AI and robotics has opened up numerous applications across various sectors. Here are some of the most significant use cases:

1. Manufacturing and Industry 4.0

AI-powered robots are at the heart of the Industry 4.0 revolution, which aims to create smart factories that are highly automated and interconnected. These robots can perform tasks such as assembly, welding, painting, and quality inspection with precision and efficiency. They can also collaborate with human workers, enhancing productivity and safety.

2. Healthcare

AI-driven robots are transforming healthcare by assisting with surgeries, rehabilitation, and patient care. Robotic surgical systems, like the da Vinci system, allow surgeons to carry out minimally invasive operations with greater accuracy. Robotic exoskeletons help patients regain mobility after injuries, while robotic companions provide emotional support to the elderly.

3. Agriculture

In agriculture, AI-powered robots are being used for tasks such as planting, harvesting, and monitoring crops. These robots can analyze soil conditions, detect pests, and optimize irrigation, leading to increased yields and reduced environmental impact.

4. Logistics and Warehousing

The e-commerce boom has driven demand for AI-powered robots in logistics and warehousing. Autonomous mobile robots (AMRs) are used to transport goods within warehouses, while robotic arms handle sorting and packaging. Companies like Amazon and Alibaba rely heavily on these technologies to meet the growing demand for fast and efficient delivery.

5. Disaster Response

AI-powered robots are playing a critical role in disaster response by performing tasks that are too dangerous for humans. For example, robots equipped with cameras and sensors can search for survivors in collapsed buildings, while drones can assess damage and deliver supplies to inaccessible areas.

6. *Space Exploration*

Robots have long been used in space exploration, but AI is taking their capabilities to new heights. NASA's Mars rovers, for instance, use AI to navigate the Martian terrain and conduct scientific experiments. AI also enables robots to repair satellites and build structures in space.

7. *Retail and Hospitality*

In retail, AI-powered robots are being used for tasks such as inventory management, customer service, and even checkout processes. In hospitality, robots are serving food, cleaning rooms, and providing concierge services, enhancing the guest experience.

Challenges and Ethical Considerations

While the integration of AI into robotics offers immense potential, it also presents significant challenges and ethical considerations. Below are some of the key issues that must be addressed:

1. Technical Challenges

- Complexity of Real-World Environments: Robots operating in unstructured environments, such as homes or outdoor spaces, face challenges related to perception, navigation, and interaction. These environments are often unpredictable and require robots to adapt in real-time.

- Energy Efficiency: AI algorithms, particularly deep learning models, require significant computational resources, which can be a challenge for robots with limited power supplies.

- Safety and Reliability: Ensuring the safety and reliability of AI-powered robots is critical, especially in applications such as healthcare and autonomous vehicles. Failures or errors can have serious consequences.

2. Ethical and Social Implications

- Job Displacement: The widespread adoption of AI-powered robots could lead to job displacement in certain sectors, particularly those involving repetitive or manual labor. This raises concerns about economic inequality and the need for workforce reskilling.

- Privacy Concerns: Robots equipped with cameras and sensors can collect vast amounts of data, raising concerns about privacy and data security. For example, domestic robots could inadvertently record sensitive information about their users.

- Bias and Fairness: AI algorithms can perpetuate biases present in the data they are trained on, leading to unfair or discriminatory outcomes. This is particularly concerning in applications such as hiring robots or law enforcement.

- Autonomy and Accountability: As robots become more autonomous, questions arise about accountability in the event of accidents or errors. Who should be held accountable when an AI-driven robot causes damage?

3. Regulatory and Legal Challenges

The rapid advancement of AI in robotics has outpaced the development of regulatory frameworks. Governments and organizations must establish guidelines and standards to ensure the safe and ethical use of AI-powered robots. This includes addressing issues such as liability, data protection, and interoperability.

The Future of AI in Robotics

The future of AI in robotics is both exciting and uncertain. As technology continues to evolve, we can expect to see even more sophisticated and capable robots that blur the line between the physical and digital worlds. Below are some trends and possibilities for the future:

1. *Human-Robot Collaboration*

The future will likely see increased collaboration between humans and robots, with AI enabling seamless interaction and cooperation. Cobots will become more common in workplaces, assisting humans with tasks that require precision, strength, or endurance.

2. *Swarm Robotics*

Swarm robotics involves the coordination of multiple robots to achieve a common goal. Inspired by the behavior of social insects, such as ants and bees, swarm robotics has applications in areas such as search and rescue, agriculture, and environmental monitoring.

3. Emotional AI

Advances in emotional AI, or affective computing, will enable robots to recognize and respond to human emotions. This capability will enhance the effectiveness of robots in applications such as healthcare, education, and customer service.

4. Self-Learning Robots

Future robots will be capable of self-learning, allowing them to acquire new skills and adapt to new environments without human intervention. This will make robots more versatile and reduce the need for extensive programming.

5. Ethical and Inclusive Design

As AI-powered robots become more integrated into society, there will be a growing emphasis on ethical and inclusive design. This includes ensuring that robots are accessible to people with disabilities and that they are designed to promote social good.

6. Integration with Other Technologies

AI-powered robots will increasingly be integrated with other emerging technologies, such as the Internet of Things (IoT), 5G, and augmented reality (AR). This convergence will enable new applications and enhance the capabilities of robots.

Conclusion

AI in robotics represents a paradigm shift in how we interact with technology and the world around us. By bridging the gap between the physical and digital worlds, AI-powered robots are transforming industries, enhancing productivity, and improving quality of life. However, this transformation also presents challenges that must be addressed, from technical limitations to ethical concerns.

As we look to the future, it is essential to approach the development and deployment of AI-powered robots with a focus on collaboration, inclusivity, and responsibility. By doing so, we can harness the potential of this technology to create a better, more connected world. The journey ahead is complex, but with thoughtful planning and innovation, AI in robotics has the potential to revolutionize our lives in ways we are only beginning to imagine.

4. AI and Space Exploration: Pushing the Boundaries of Discovery

The Future of AI in Space

AI and Space Exploration: Pushing the Boundaries of Discovery

Space exploration has always been a testament to humanity's curiosity, ingenuity, and desire to push the boundaries of what is possible. From the first satellite launched into orbit to the recent Mars rover missions, space exploration has evolved significantly over the decades. Today, Artificial Intelligence (AI) is playing an increasingly critical role in advancing our understanding of the cosmos. By enabling autonomous decision-making, enhancing data analysis, and powering advanced robotics, AI is revolutionizing how we explore space. This essay delves into the role of AI in space exploration, its applications in missions and satellite data analysis, its use in planetary exploration and robotics, the challenges it presents, and its future potential.

How AI is Used in Space Missions and Satellite Data Analysis

AI is transforming space missions and satellite operations by enabling faster, more accurate, and more efficient processes. From mission planning to data interpretation, AI is becoming an indispensable tool for space agencies and private companies alike. Below are some key ways AI is being used in space missions and satellite data analysis:

1. Autonomous Navigation and Decision-Making
One of the most significant contributions of AI to space exploration is its ability to enable autonomous navigation and decision-making. Spacecraft and rovers operating in distant

environments, such as Mars or the Moon, cannot rely on real-time human control due to communication delays. AI algorithms allow these systems to navigate terrain, avoid obstacles, and make decisions independently. For example, NASA's Perseverance rover uses AI to autonomously navigate the Martian surface, selecting the safest and most efficient paths.

2. Data Processing and Analysis

Space missions generate vast amounts of data, from high-resolution images to complex sensor readings. AI, particularly machine learning, is used to process and analyze this data quickly and accurately. For instance, AI algorithms can identify patterns in satellite imagery, such as changes in Earth's surface or the presence of exoplanets in distant star systems. This capability is crucial for making sense of the enormous datasets collected by missions like the Hubble Space Telescope and the James Webb Space Telescope.

3. Predictive Maintenance

Satellites and spacecraft are complex systems that require constant monitoring to ensure optimal performance. AI-powered predictive maintenance systems analyze data from sensors to detect anomalies and predict potential failures before they occur. This reduces downtime, extends the lifespan of equipment, and minimizes the risk of mission failure.

4. Mission Planning and Optimization

AI is also used to optimize mission planning, from trajectory calculations to resource allocation. For example, AI algorithms can determine the most efficient routes for spacecraft, taking into account factors such as fuel consumption and gravitational forces. This ensures that missions are executed with maximum efficiency and minimal risk.

5. *Real-Time Monitoring and Control*

AI enables real-time monitoring and control of spacecraft and satellites, allowing operators to respond quickly to unexpected events. For example, AI systems can detect and mitigate issues such as solar flares or equipment malfunctions, ensuring the safety and success of missions.

Applications of AI in Planetary Exploration and Space Robotics

AI is at the forefront of planetary exploration and space robotics, enabling machines to perform tasks that were once thought impossible. Below are some of the most exciting applications of AI in these fields:

1. *Autonomous Rovers*

Autonomous rovers, such as NASA's Curiosity and Perseverance, rely on AI to navigate and conduct scientific experiments on distant planets. These rovers use AI algorithms to analyze terrain, avoid obstacles, and select targets for analysis. For example, Perseverance's AI-powered system can identify rocks and soil samples that may contain signs of ancient microbial life.

2. Space Robotics

AI-powered robots are being used for a variety of tasks in space, from repairing satellites to assembling structures. For instance, the Robotic Refueling Mission (RRM) demonstrated the use of AI-driven robots to refuel and repair satellites in orbit. Similarly, AI-powered robotic arms are being developed to construct habitats on the Moon and Mars.

3. Planetary Mapping and Exploration

AI is used to create detailed maps of planetary surfaces, enabling scientists to study geological features and plan future missions. For example, AI algorithms have been used to map the surface of Mars, identifying potential landing sites and areas of scientific interest.

4. Sample Analysis

AI is revolutionizing the way samples collected during space missions are analyzed. Machine learning algorithms can identify minerals, organic compounds, and other materials in samples, providing valuable insights into the composition and history of planets and moons.

5. Swarm Robotics

Swarm robotics involves the coordination of multiple robots to achieve a common goal. In space exploration, swarm robotics could be used to explore large areas, such as the surface of a planet or the interior of a cave. AI algorithms enable these robots to communicate, collaborate, and adapt to changing conditions.

Challenges in AI-Driven Space Exploration

While AI offers immense potential for space exploration, it also presents significant challenges that must be addressed. Below are some of the key challenges in AI-driven space exploration:

1. Technical Limitations

- Computational Constraints: Spacecraft and rovers have limited computational resources, which can restrict the complexity of AI algorithms that can be used.
- Energy Efficiency: AI algorithms, particularly deep learning models, require significant amounts of energy,

which can be a challenge for missions with limited power supplies.

- Reliability and Robustness: AI systems must be highly reliable and robust to operate in the harsh and unpredictable environments of space.

2. *Communication Delays*

Communication delays between Earth and distant spacecraft can make real-time control impossible. While AI enables autonomy, it also requires careful design to ensure that systems can operate effectively without human intervention.

3. *Data Management*

Space missions generate vast amounts of data, which can be challenging to store, transmit, and analyze. AI systems must be designed to handle these large datasets efficiently.

4. *Ethical and Legal Considerations*

The use of AI in space exploration raises ethical and legal questions, such as who is responsible for decisions made by autonomous systems and how to ensure that AI is used responsibly.

5. *Interdisciplinary Collaboration*

AI-driven space exploration requires collaboration between experts in AI, robotics, astronomy, and other fields. Bridging the gap between these disciplines can be challenging but is essential for success.

The Future of AI in Space

The potential for AI in space exploration is brimming with thrilling opportunities. As technology progresses, AI will become even more integral to expanding the frontiers of discovery. Here are some emerging trends and future possibilities:

1. Advanced Autonomous Systems

Future missions will rely on even more advanced autonomous systems capable of making complex decisions and adapting to unforeseen challenges. These systems will enable missions to explore more distant and challenging environments, such as the moons of Jupiter and Saturn.

2. AI-Powered Space Habitats

AI will play a key role in the development of space habitats, from designing and constructing structures to managing life support systems. AI-powered robots could be used to build and maintain habitats on the Moon and Mars, enabling long-term human presence in space.

3. Interplanetary Internet

AI could enable the creation of an interplanetary internet, allowing for seamless communication between Earth, Mars, and other destinations. This would facilitate data sharing, remote control of systems, and collaboration between scientists and engineers.

4. *AI-Driven Space Mining*

AI-powered robots could be used to mine asteroids and other celestial bodies for valuable resources, such as water and rare metals. This could support future space missions and even provide resources for use on Earth.

5. *Exploration of Extreme Environments*

AI will enable the exploration of extreme environments, such as the subsurface oceans of Europa and Enceladus. AI-powered robots could navigate these environments, collect samples, and search for signs of life.

6. *Collaboration Between Humans and AI*

The next phase of space exploration is expected to feature a strong partnership between humans and AI. AI systems will assist astronauts with tasks, provide real-time insights, and enhance decision-making, enabling more ambitious missions.

7. *Ethical and Inclusive Exploration*

As AI becomes more integrated into space exploration, there will be a growing emphasis on ethical and inclusive practices. This includes ensuring that AI systems are transparent, fair, and designed to benefit all of humanity.

Conclusion

AI is revolutionizing space exploration, enabling us to push the boundaries of discovery and achieve what was once thought impossible. From autonomous rovers on Mars to AI-powered satellites orbiting Earth, AI is transforming how we explore and understand the cosmos. However, this transformation also presents challenges that must be addressed, from technical limitations to ethical considerations.

As we look to the future, it is essential to approach the development and deployment of AI in space exploration with a focus on collaboration, innovation, and responsibility. By doing so, we can harness the potential of AI to unlock the mysteries of the universe and inspire future generations to reach for the stars. The journey ahead is filled with challenges, but with the power of AI, the possibilities are limitless.

Section 6: Creative and Immersive AI

1. AI in Creative Industries: Art, Music, and Content Creation

The creative industries have always been at the forefront of innovation, constantly evolving with the advent of new technologies. In recent years, artificial intelligence (AI) has emerged as a transformative force, reshaping the way art, music, and content are created, consumed, and distributed. From AI-generated paintings and music compositions to automated content creation and design, the integration of AI into creative processes is revolutionizing the industry. This chapter explores the impact of AI on creative industries, focusing on AI-generated art, music, and literature, its applications in film, gaming, and design, the ethical and copyright challenges it poses, and the future of AI in creative industries.

AI-Generated Art, Music, and Literature

AI-Generated Art

Art has always been a reflection of human creativity, emotion, and expression. However, with the advent of AI, the boundaries of what constitutes art are being pushed further than ever before. AI-generated art refers to artworks created with the assistance of artificial intelligence algorithms, which can analyze vast amounts of data, learn from it, and generate new, original pieces of art.

One of the most notable examples of AI-generated art is the work of the AI program "DeepArt," which uses neural networks to transform photographs into artworks that mimic the styles of renowned artists such as Van Gogh, Picasso, and Monet. Another example is "GANs" (Generative Adversarial Networks), which consist of two neural networks—the generator and the discriminator—that work together to create realistic images. GANs have been used to generate everything from realistic portraits to abstract art.

AI-generated art is not limited to visual art. It also extends to other forms of creative expression, such as digital sculptures and installations. For instance, the AI program "AICAN" has been used to create digital sculptures that are both aesthetically pleasing and conceptually profound. These sculptures are generated by analyzing thousands of existing artworks and learning the underlying patterns and styles, allowing the AI to create new, original pieces.

The rise of AI-generated art has sparked a debate about the role of the artist in the creative process. Some argue that AI is merely a tool that artists can use to enhance their creativity, while others believe that AI has the potential to replace human artists altogether. Regardless of where one stands on this debate, it is clear that AI-generated art is here to stay and will continue to evolve as AI technology advances.

AI-Generated Music

Music is another creative domain that has been significantly impacted by AI. AI-generated music refers to compositions created with the assistance of artificial intelligence algorithms, which can analyze musical patterns, harmonies, and rhythms to generate new, original pieces of music.

One of the most well-known examples of AI-generated music is the work of the AI program "AIVA" (Artificial Intelligence Virtual Artist), which composes original music in various genres, including classical, jazz, and pop. AIVA analyzes thousands of musical compositions to learn the underlying patterns and structures, allowing it to create new pieces that are both original and stylistically consistent.

Another example is "Amper Music," an AI-powered music composition tool that allows users to create custom music tracks by selecting a genre, mood, and tempo. Amper Music uses machine learning algorithms to generate music that is tailored to the user's specifications, making it a valuable tool for content creators, filmmakers, and game developers.

AI-generated music is not limited to instrumental compositions. It also extends to vocal music, with AI programs like "Jukedeck" and "OpenAI's MuseNet" capable of generating lyrics and melodies for songs. These programs analyze vast amounts of text and musical data to create lyrics that are both meaningful and emotionally resonant.

The rise of AI-generated music has raised questions about the role of the composer in the creative process. Some argue that AI is merely a tool that composers can use to enhance their creativity, while others believe that AI has the potential to replace human composers altogether. Regardless of where one stands on this debate, it is clear that AI-generated music is becoming increasingly sophisticated and will continue to play a significant role in the music industry.

AI-Generated Literature

Literature, like art and music, is a form of creative expression that has been impacted by AI. AI-generated literature refers to written works created with the assistance of artificial intelligence algorithms, which can analyze text, learn from it, and generate new, original pieces of writing.

One of the most notable examples of AI-generated literature is the work of the AI program "GPT-3" (Generative Pre-trained Transformer 3), developed by OpenAI. GPT-3 is an advanced language model capable of producing text that resembles human writing when provided with a prompt. It has been used to create everything from short stories and poems to news articles and essays. GPT-3's ability to generate coherent and contextually relevant text has made it a valuable tool for writers, journalists, and content creators.

Another example is "Sudowrite," an AI-powered writing assistant that helps writers generate ideas, improve their writing, and overcome writer's block. Sudowrite uses machine learning algorithms to analyze text and provide suggestions for improving grammar, style, and structure. It can also generate new content based on a given prompt, making it a valuable tool for writers looking to enhance their creativity.

AI-generated literature is not limited to fiction. It also extends to non-fiction, with AI programs like "Quill" and "Wordsmith" capable of generating reports, summaries, and data-driven articles. These programs analyze vast amounts of data and use natural language processing (NLP) algorithms to create written content that is both accurate and informative.

The rise of AI-generated literature has sparked a debate about the role of the writer in the creative process. Some argue that AI is merely a tool that writers can use to enhance their creativity, while others believe that AI has the potential to replace human writers altogether. Regardless of where one stands on this debate, it is clear that AI-generated literature is becoming increasingly sophisticated and will continue to play a significant role in the publishing industry.

Applications of AI in Film, Gaming, and Design

AI in Film

The film industry has always been at the forefront of technological innovation, and AI is no exception. AI is being utilized in multiple stages of filmmaking, including script creation, pre-visualization, post-production, and distribution.

One of the most significant applications of AI in film is in the area of scriptwriting. AI programs like "ScriptBook" and "LargoAI" analyze scripts and predict their potential success at the box office. These programs use machine learning algorithms to analyze factors such as plot structure, character development, and dialogue, providing filmmakers with valuable insights into how to improve their scripts.

AI is also being used in pre-visualization, the process of creating rough versions of scenes before they are filmed. AI-powered tools like "Arraiy" and "Cinelytic" allow filmmakers to create realistic 3D models of sets, characters, and props, enabling them to visualize scenes and make adjustments before filming begins. This not only saves time and money but also allows filmmakers to experiment with different creative ideas.

In post-production, AI is being used to enhance visual effects (VFX), color grading, and editing. AI-powered tools like "Adobe's Sensei" and "DaVinci Resolve" use machine learning algorithms to automate repetitive tasks, such as rotoscoping and color correction, allowing filmmakers to focus on more creative aspects of post-production. AI is also being used to create realistic CGI characters and environments, as seen in films like "The Lion King" (2019) and "Avatar" (2009).

AI is also playing a role in film distribution and marketing. AI-powered platforms like "Pilot" and "Cinelytic" analyze audience data and predict the potential success of a film in different markets. This allows filmmakers to tailor their marketing strategies and distribution plans to maximize box office revenue.

AI in Gaming

The gaming industry has been quick to adopt AI technology, using it to enhance gameplay, create realistic environments, and develop intelligent non-player characters (NPCs).

One of the most significant applications of AI in gaming is in the area of procedural content generation. AI algorithms are used to generate game levels, maps, and environments dynamically, providing players with a unique experience each time they play. Games like "No Man's Sky" and "Minecraft" use procedural generation to create vast, open worlds that are different every time the game is played.

AI is also being used to create intelligent NPCs that can interact with players in a more realistic and engaging way. AI-powered NPCs can learn from player behavior, adapt to different situations, and make decisions based on complex algorithms. This creates a more immersive gaming experience, as players feel like they are interacting with real characters rather than pre-programmed bots.

In addition to enhancing gameplay, AI is also being used to improve game design and development. AI-powered tools like "Unity's ML-Agents" and "Unreal Engine's AI Toolkit" allow game developers to create more sophisticated AI systems, test game mechanics, and optimize performance. This not only speeds up the development process but also allows developers to create more complex and engaging games.

AI is also contributing to game promotion and enhancing player interaction. AI-powered platforms like "PlayFab" and "GameAnalytics" analyze player data and provide insights into player behavior, preferences, and engagement. This allows game developers to tailor their games to meet the needs of their target audience, increasing player retention and revenue.

AI in Design

The design industry has also been impacted by AI, with AI-powered tools being used to enhance creativity, streamline workflows, and improve the quality of design work.

One of the most significant applications of AI in design is in the area of graphic design. AI-powered tools like "Canva" and "Adobe's Sensei" allow designers to create professional-quality designs quickly and easily. These tools use machine learning algorithms to analyze design trends, suggest color palettes, and generate layouts, making it easier for designers to create visually appealing designs.

AI is also being used in web design, with AI-powered platforms like "Wix ADI" and "Bookmark" allowing users to create websites without any coding knowledge. These platforms use AI algorithms to analyze user preferences and generate custom website designs that are tailored to the user's needs. This not only saves time but also allows users to create professional-quality websites with minimal effort.

In product design, AI is being used to optimize designs and improve functionality. AI-powered tools like "Autodesk's Dreamcatcher" and "SolidWorks' Generative Design" allow designers to input design constraints and goals, and the AI generates multiple design options that meet those criteria. This not only speeds up the design process but also allows designers to explore new creative possibilities.

AI is also playing a role in fashion design, with AI-powered tools like "Stitch Fix" and "IBM's Watson" being used to analyze fashion trends, predict consumer preferences, and generate new designs. These tools use machine learning algorithms to analyze vast amounts of data, allowing fashion designers to create designs that are both stylish and marketable.

Ethical and Copyright Challenges in AI Creativity

As AI continues to play a significant role in creative industries, it raises important ethical and copyright challenges that need to be addressed. These challenges include issues related to authorship, ownership, and the potential for AI to perpetuate biases and inequalities.

Authorship and Ownership

One of the most significant ethical challenges posed by AI-generated creativity is the question of authorship and ownership. When an AI creates a piece of art, music, or literature, who owns the rights to that creation? Should accountability lie with the AI's creator, the individual who trained it, or the AI itself?

Currently, copyright law does not recognize AI as a legal entity, which means that the rights to AI-generated works typically belong to the person or organization that created the AI. However, this raises questions about the role of human creativity in the creative process. If an AI generates a piece of art or music, can it truly be considered original, or is it merely a derivative work based on the data it was trained on?

This issue becomes even more complex when considering collaborative works created by humans and AI. For example, if a musician uses an AI program to compose a piece of music, who owns the rights to that composition? Is it the musician, the AI programmer, or both? These questions highlight the need for a new legal framework that addresses the unique challenges posed by AI-generated creativity.

Bias and Inequality

Another ethical challenge posed by AI-generated creativity is the potential for AI to perpetuate biases and inequalities. AI systems learn from massive datasets, which may contain biased or prejudiced information. If this data is not carefully curated, the AI may learn and replicate these biases in its creative output.

For example, if an AI is trained on a dataset of predominantly male-authored literature, it may generate text that reflects a male perspective, potentially excluding or marginalizing female voices. Similarly, if an AI is trained on a dataset of predominantly Western art, it may generate art that reflects Western aesthetics, potentially excluding or marginalizing non-Western artistic traditions.

This raises important questions about the role of AI in shaping cultural narratives and the potential for AI to reinforce existing power structures and inequalities. To address these challenges, it is essential to ensure that AI algorithms are trained on diverse and representative datasets and that the creative output of AI is carefully monitored for bias and discrimination.

Transparency and Accountability

Transparency and accountability are also important ethical considerations when it comes to AI-generated creativity. As AI becomes more integrated into creative industries, it is essential to ensure that the creative process is transparent and that the role of AI is clearly disclosed.

For example, if a piece of music is generated by an AI, should the listener be informed that the music was not composed by a human? Similarly, if a piece of art is created by an AI, should the viewer be informed that the artwork was not created by a human artist? These questions highlight the need for clear guidelines and standards for disclosing the role of AI in creative works.

In addition to transparency, accountability is also an important consideration. If an AI generates a piece of content that is harmful or offensive, who is responsible for that content? Should accountability lie with the AI's creator, the individual who trained it, or the AI itself? These questions highlight the need for a clear framework for holding individuals and organizations accountable for the creative output of AI.

The Future of AI in Creative Industries

As AI technology continues to advance, its impact on creative industries is likely to grow. In the future, we can expect to see even more sophisticated AI-generated art, music, and literature, as well as new applications of AI in film, gaming, and design.

One of the most exciting possibilities for the future of AI in creative industries is the potential for AI to collaborate with human creators. Rather than replacing human creativity, AI has the potential to enhance it, providing new tools and techniques that allow creators to push the boundaries of their imagination. For example, AI could be used to generate new ideas, suggest creative solutions, and automate repetitive tasks, allowing creators to focus on the more creative aspects of their work.

Another possibility is the development of AI-powered creative platforms that allow anyone to create art, music, and literature, regardless of their skill level. These platforms could democratize creativity, making it accessible to a wider audience and allowing more people to express themselves creatively.

However, as AI becomes more integrated into creative industries, it will be essential to address the ethical and copyright challenges it poses. This will require a collaborative effort between policymakers, industry leaders, and creators to develop new legal frameworks, guidelines, and standards that ensure AI is used responsibly and ethically.

In conclusion, AI is transforming the creative industries in profound and exciting ways. From AI-generated art, music, and literature to new applications in film, gaming, and design, AI is reshaping the way we create, consume, and distribute creative content. As we look to the future, it is essential to embrace the potential of AI while also addressing the challenges it poses, ensuring that AI is used to enhance human creativity rather than replace it.

2. AI and the Metaverse: Building Immersive Digital Worlds

The concept of the Metaverse—a collective virtual shared space created by the convergence of virtually enhanced physical and digital reality—has captured the imagination of technologists, entrepreneurs, and futurists alike. As the Metaverse evolves, artificial intelligence (AI) is emerging as a critical enabler, shaping how these immersive digital worlds are created, managed, and experienced. From designing lifelike virtual environments to powering intelligent avatars and virtual economies, AI is at the heart of the Metaverse's development. This chapter explores the role of

AI in building the Metaverse, its applications in virtual economies, avatars, and social interactions, the challenges in AI-driven Metaverse development, and the future of AI in this burgeoning digital frontier.

The Impact of AI on Building and Overseeing the Metaverse

Designing Immersive Virtual Environments

At the core of the Metaverse is the creation of immersive, interactive, and dynamic virtual environments. AI plays a pivotal role in designing these environments, making them more realistic, engaging, and responsive to user interactions.

Procedural Content Generation

AI-driven procedural content generation (PCG) is a key technology for building the vast, interconnected worlds of the Metaverse. PCG uses algorithms to automatically create content such as landscapes, buildings, and even entire cities. For example, AI can generate realistic terrain, vegetation, and weather systems, reducing the need for manual design and enabling the creation of expansive, diverse virtual worlds. Games like No Man's Sky have already demonstrated the potential of PCG, using AI to create billions of unique planets for players to explore.

Real-Time Adaptation and Personalization

AI enables virtual environments to adapt in real-time to user behavior and preferences. Machine learning algorithms can analyze user interactions and adjust the environment accordingly, creating a personalized experience for each user. For instance, if a user frequently visits a specific type of virtual location, the AI can generate similar environments or recommend new areas that align with their interests. This level of personalization enhances user engagement and makes the Metaverse feel more alive and responsive.

Dynamic World-Building

AI can also manage dynamic world-building, where the virtual environment evolves over time based on user actions and external inputs. For example, AI can simulate the growth of a virtual city, with buildings, roads, and infrastructure developing in response to user activities. This creates a sense of continuity and progression, making the Metaverse feel like a living, breathing world.

Managing Complex Systems and Interactions

The Metaverse is not just a collection of static environments; it is a complex ecosystem of interconnected systems, including virtual economies, social networks, and user-generated content. AI is essential for managing these systems and ensuring they operate smoothly and efficiently.

Scalability and Resource Management

As the Metaverse grows, it will need to support millions—or even billions—of users simultaneously. AI can optimize resource allocation, ensuring that computational power, bandwidth, and storage are used efficiently. For example, AI can predict user demand and allocate server resources dynamically, reducing latency and improving performance. This is particularly important for maintaining a seamless experience in large-scale virtual events or crowded virtual spaces.

Content Moderation and Safety

With user-generated content playing a significant role in the Metaverse, AI is crucial for moderating content and ensuring a safe and inclusive environment. AI-powered tools can detect and remove inappropriate content, such as hate speech, harassment, or explicit material, in real-time. Natural language processing (NLP) algorithms can analyze text and voice chats, while computer vision algorithms can monitor visual content. These tools help maintain a positive and respectful community within the Metaverse.

Security and Fraud Prevention

The Metaverse will also need robust security measures to protect users from fraud, hacking, and other malicious activities. AI can enhance security by detecting unusual patterns of behavior, identifying potential threats, and preventing unauthorized access. For example, AI can analyze transaction data in virtual economies to detect fraudulent activities or monitor user accounts for signs of compromise.

Applications of AI in Virtual Economies, Avatars, and Social Interactions

Virtual Economies

Virtual economies are a cornerstone of the Metaverse, enabling users to buy, sell, and trade virtual goods and services. AI plays a critical role in managing these economies, ensuring they are fair, efficient, and sustainable.

Dynamic Pricing and Market Analysis

AI can analyze supply and demand dynamics in virtual economies, adjusting prices in real-time to reflect market conditions. For example, if a particular virtual item becomes scarce, AI can increase its price to balance supply and demand. Conversely, if an item is overabundant, AI can lower its price to stimulate sales. This dynamic pricing model ensures that virtual economies remain balanced and responsive to user behavior.

Fraud Detection and Prevention

Virtual economies are vulnerable to fraud, such as counterfeit goods, money laundering, and unauthorized transactions. AI can detect and prevent these activities by analyzing transaction patterns and identifying anomalies. For example, if a user suddenly starts making large, unusual transactions, AI can flag the activity for further investigation. This helps maintain the integrity of virtual economies and protects users from financial losses.

Personalized Recommendations

AI can enhance user experiences in virtual economies by providing personalized recommendations. For example, if a user frequently purchases virtual clothing, AI can suggest new items or brands that match their style. Similarly, if a user is interested in virtual real estate, AI can recommend properties that meet their preferences and budget. These personalized recommendations increase user engagement and drive economic activity within the Metaverse.

Avatars

Avatars are the digital representations of users in the Metaverse, serving as their primary means of interaction and self-expression. AI is transforming how avatars are created, customized, and animated, making them more lifelike and responsive.

Avatar Creation and Customization

AI-powered tools enable users to create highly detailed and personalized avatars. For example, AI can analyze a user's facial features and generate a 3D model that closely resembles their real-life appearance. Users can further customize their avatars by selecting hairstyles, clothing, and accessories, with AI providing real-time previews and suggestions. This level of customization allows users to express their identity and personality in the Metaverse.

Realistic Animation and Behavior

AI is also used to animate avatars, making their movements and expressions more realistic and natural. Machine learning algorithms can analyze motion capture data and generate animations that mimic human behavior. For example, AI can simulate facial expressions, body language, and even subtle gestures, making avatars feel more lifelike. Additionally, AI can enable avatars to respond to user inputs in real-time, such as nodding in agreement or smiling in response to a joke.

Emotional Intelligence and Social Interaction

AI can enhance the social capabilities of avatars by enabling them to recognize and respond to human emotions. For example, AI-powered avatars can analyze a user's voice tone, facial expressions, and text inputs to infer their emotional state. Based on this analysis, the avatar can adjust its behavior, such as offering comfort during a difficult conversation or celebrating a user's achievements. This emotional intelligence makes social interactions in the Metaverse more meaningful and engaging.

Social Interactions

Social interactions are at the heart of the Metaverse, enabling users to connect, collaborate, and build relationships in virtual spaces. AI is enhancing these interactions by enabling more natural and immersive communication.

Natural Language Processing (NLP)

AI-powered NLP enables real-time translation and transcription of conversations in the Metaverse, breaking down language barriers and enabling global communication. For example, if two users speak different languages, AI can translate their speech in real-time, allowing them to communicate seamlessly. Additionally, AI can transcribe voice chats into text, making conversations accessible to users with hearing impairments.

Context-Aware Interactions

AI can analyze the context of social interactions, enabling more relevant and meaningful conversations. For example, if users are discussing a specific topic, AI can provide contextual information or suggest related topics to enhance the discussion. Similarly, AI can analyze the tone and content of conversations to detect conflicts or misunderstandings, offering suggestions for resolving disputes or improving communication.

Virtual Social Assistants

AI-powered virtual assistants can enhance social interactions by providing support and guidance. For example, a virtual assistant can help users navigate the Metaverse, find friends, or join social events. These assistants can also provide personalized recommendations, such as suggesting new connections or activities based on a user's interests. By facilitating social interactions, AI-powered assistants help users build meaningful relationships in the Metaverse.

Challenges in AI-Driven Metaverse Development

While AI holds immense potential for the Metaverse, its development is not without challenges. These challenges include technical limitations, ethical concerns, and the need for robust governance frameworks.

Technical Challenges

Computational Complexity

The Metaverse requires massive computational resources to support real-time rendering, AI processing, and user interactions. AI algorithms, particularly those involving deep learning, are computationally intensive and require significant processing power. Ensuring that the Metaverse can scale to accommodate millions of users while maintaining performance is a major technical challenge.

Data Privacy and Security

The Metaverse relies on vast amounts of user data, including personal information, behavioral data, and financial transactions.

Ensuring the privacy and security of this data is critical to building user trust. AI systems must be designed with robust encryption, anonymization, and access control mechanisms to protect user data from breaches and misuse.

Interoperability

The Metaverse is imagined as a linked network of platforms, apps, and services. Achieving interoperability between these systems is a significant technical challenge, particularly when it comes to AI-driven features. For example, ensuring that AI-powered avatars can seamlessly transition between different virtual environments requires standardized protocols and APIs.

Ethical and Social Challenges

Bias and Discrimination

AI systems reflect the biases present in their training data. If the data includes biases, the AI might reinforce or magnify these biases within the Metaverse. For example, AI-powered avatars or content moderation systems may exhibit racial, gender, or cultural biases, leading to discriminatory outcomes. Addressing these biases requires diverse and representative training data, as well as ongoing monitoring and evaluation of AI systems.

Digital Addiction and Mental Health

The immersive nature of the Metaverse raises concerns about digital addiction and its impact on mental health. AI-driven personalization and engagement strategies, while enhancing user experiences, may also contribute to excessive use and dependency. Ensuring that the Metaverse promotes healthy usage patterns and provides support for users at risk of addiction is an important ethical consideration.

Ownership and Intellectual Property

The Metaverse blurs the lines between physical and digital ownership, raising complex questions about intellectual property rights. For example, who owns the rights to AI-generated content, such as virtual art or music? How are these rights enforced in a decentralized, user-driven environment? Developing clear legal frameworks to address these issues is essential for the sustainable growth of the Metaverse.

Governance and Regulation

Decentralization vs. Centralization

The Metaverse is often envisioned as a decentralized ecosystem, where users have greater control over their data and experiences. However, achieving decentralization while maintaining security, scalability, and interoperability is a significant challenge. Balancing the benefits of decentralization with the need for centralized governance and regulation is a key issue for Metaverse development.

Ethical AI Governance

As AI becomes more integrated into the Metaverse, there is a growing need for ethical AI governance. This includes establishing guidelines for the responsible use of AI, ensuring transparency and accountability, and protecting user rights. Developing international standards and regulatory frameworks for AI in the Metaverse is essential to address these challenges.

The Future of AI in the Metaverse

The future of AI in the Metaverse is both exciting and uncertain. As AI technology continues to advance, it will play an increasingly central role in shaping the Metaverse, enabling new possibilities for creativity, interaction, and innovation.

AI-Driven Creativity and Innovation

AI will empower users to create and innovate in ways that were previously unimaginable. From AI-generated art and music to user-designed virtual worlds, the Metaverse will become a hub of creativity and collaboration. AI will also enable new forms of storytelling, gaming, and entertainment, pushing the boundaries of what is possible in digital spaces.

Enhanced Social and Economic Interactions

AI will enhance social and economic interactions in the Metaverse, making them more immersive, personalized, and meaningful. Virtual economies will become more dynamic and inclusive, while social interactions will become more natural and emotionally intelligent. AI-powered avatars and assistants will enable users to connect and collaborate in new ways, fostering a sense of community and belonging.

Ethical and Inclusive Development

As the Metaverse evolves, it will be essential to prioritize ethical and inclusive development. This includes addressing biases, ensuring data privacy, and promoting healthy usage patterns. By embedding ethical principles into the design and governance of the Metaverse, we can create a digital world that is fair, inclusive, and beneficial for all.

Collaboration and Interoperability

The future of the Metaverse will depend on collaboration and interoperability between platforms, developers, and users. AI will play a key role in enabling seamless integration and communication between different systems, creating a unified and interconnected digital ecosystem. By working together, we can build a Metaverse that is greater than the sum of its parts.

In conclusion, AI is a transformative force in the development of the Metaverse, enabling the creation of immersive, dynamic, and interconnected digital worlds. From virtual economies and avatars to social interactions and content creation, AI is reshaping how we experience and interact with the Metaverse. However, realizing the full potential of AI in the Metaverse requires addressing technical, ethical, and governance challenges. By embracing innovation while prioritizing ethical and inclusive development, we can build a Metaverse that enriches our lives and expands the boundaries of human creativity and connection.

Glossary

A

1. Artificial Intelligence (AI): The simulation of human intelligence in machines programmed to think, learn, and make decisions.

2. Algorithm: A set of rules or instructions given to an AI system to perform tasks or solve problems.

3. AGI (Artificial General Intelligence): AI that possesses the ability to understand, learn, and apply knowledge across a wide range of tasks at a human level.

4. AI Ethics: The study of moral issues and implications related to AI development and deployment.

5. Autonomous Systems: Machines or systems capable of performing tasks without human intervention.

6. AI Bias: Unintended prejudice in AI systems due to biased data or algorithms.

7. AI Governance: Policies and frameworks to regulate the development and use of AI technologies.

8. AIaaS (AI as a Service): Cloud-based platforms offering AI tools and services on demand.

9. Adversarial AI: Techniques used to exploit vulnerabilities in AI systems, such as adversarial attacks.

10. Augmented Intelligence: AI systems designed to enhance human decision-making rather than replace it.

B

1. Big Data: Extremely large datasets analyzed computationally to reveal patterns and trends.

2. Blockchain: A decentralized digital ledger technology that can enhance AI transparency and security.

3. Bots: Automated software applications that perform tasks, such as chatbots or web crawlers.

4. Backpropagation: A training algorithm used in neural networks to minimize errors.

5. Bayesian Networks: Probabilistic graphical models used for reasoning under uncertainty.

C

1. Computer Vision: A field of AI that enables machines to interpret and analyze visual data.

2. Cognitive Computing: AI systems that mimic human thought processes to solve complex problems.

3. ChatGPT: A conversational AI model based on the GPT architecture.

4. Cybersecurity AI: AI applications designed to detect and prevent cyber threats.

5. Cloud AI: AI services hosted on cloud platforms for scalability and accessibility.

D

1. Deep Learning: A subset of machine learning using neural networks with multiple layers.

2. Data Mining: The technique of identifying patterns within extensive collections of data.

3. Digital Twin: A virtual representation of a physical object or system, often enhanced with AI.

4. Decision Trees: A machine learning model used for classification and regression tasks.

5. Diffusion Models: Generative AI models used for creating realistic images or data.

E

1. Edge AI: AI processing performed on local devices rather than centralized servers.

2. Explainable AI (XAI): AI systems designed to provide transparent and interpretable results.

3. Ensemble Learning: Combining multiple machine learning models to improve performance.

4. Expert Systems: AI systems that emulate the decision-making ability of a human expert.

5. Ethical AI: AI developed with consideration for fairness, accountability, and societal impact.

F

1. Federated Learning: A decentralized approach to training AI models across multiple devices.

2. Fuzzy Logic: A form of logic used in AI to handle approximate reasoning.

3. Facial Recognition: AI technology used to identify or verify individuals based on facial features.

4. Feature Engineering: The process of selecting and transforming variables for machine learning models.

5. Few-Shot Learning: Training AI models with minimal data.

G

1. Generative AI: AI models capable of creating new content, such as text, images, or music.

2. GPT (Generative Pre-trained Transformer): A family of large language models used for natural language processing.

3. Gradient Descent: An optimization algorithm used to minimize errors in machine learning models.

4. Graph Neural Networks (GNNs): AI models designed to process graph-structured data.

5. General Adversarial Networks (GANs): AI models where two neural networks compete to generate realistic data.

H

1. Human-in-the-Loop (HITL): AI systems that incorporate human feedback during training or operation.

2. Hyperparameters: Parameters set before training a machine learning model.

3. Heuristics: Problem-solving techniques used by AI to find approximate solutions.

4. Hybrid AI: Combining symbolic AI with machine learning for improved performance.

5. HCI (Human-Computer Interaction): The study of how humans interact with AI systems.

I

1. IoT (Internet of Things): A network of interconnected devices that can leverage AI for automation.

2. Image Recognition: AI technology used to identify objects, people, or patterns in images.

3. Inference: The process of using a trained AI model to make predictions or decisions.

4. Intent Recognition: AI systems that identify user intentions from text or speech.

5. Intelligent Automation: Combining AI with robotic process automation (RPA) to streamline workflows.

L

1. Large Language Models (LLMs): AI models trained on vast amounts of text data for natural language tasks.

2. Lidar (Light Detection and Ranging): A remote sensing technology used in AI applications like autonomous vehicles.

3. Long Short-Term Memory (LSTM): A type of recurrent neural network used for sequence prediction.

4. Lifelong Learning: AI systems that continuously learn and adapt over time.

5. Linguistic AI: AI applications focused on understanding and generating human language.

M

1. Machine Learning (ML): A subset of AI focused on training algorithms to learn from data.

2. Model Training: The process of teaching an AI system to recognize patterns or make decisions.

3. Multimodal AI: AI systems capable of processing multiple types of data, such as text, images, and audio.

4. Meta-Learning: AI systems that learn how to learn, improving their adaptability.

5. MLOps (Machine Learning Operations): Practices for deploying and maintaining machine learning models.

N

1. Natural Language Processing (NLP): AI technology used to understand and generate human language.

2. Neural Networks: Computational models inspired by the human brain, used in deep learning.

3. Neuro-Symbolic AI: Combining neural networks with symbolic reasoning for advanced problem-solving.

4. No-Code AI: Platforms enabling users to build AI applications without programming.

5. Narrow AI: AI designed for specific tasks, as opposed to general intelligence.

R

1. Reinforcement Learning: A type of machine learning where agents learn by interacting with an environment.

2. Robotics: The field of designing and programming robots, often enhanced with AI.

3. Responsible AI: AI developed with ethical considerations and societal impact in mind.

4. Real-Time AI: AI systems capable of processing and responding to data in real time.

5. Recurrent Neural Networks (RNNs): Neural networks designed for sequential data, such as time series or text.

S

1. Supervised Learning: A machine learning approach where models are trained on labeled data.

2. Swarm Intelligence: AI systems inspired by the collective behavior of decentralized systems, such as ant colonies.

3. Speech Recognition: AI technology used to convert spoken language into text.

4. Sentiment Analysis: AI techniques used to determine the emotional tone of text or speech.

5. Self-Supervised Learning: A machine learning approach where models generate their own labels from unlabeled data.

T

1. Transfer Learning: A technique where a pre-trained model is adapted for a new, related task.

2. Turing Test: A test proposed by Alan Turing to evaluate a machine's ability to exhibit intelligent behavior indistinguishable from a human.

3. Time Series Analysis: AI techniques used to analyze data points collected over time.

4. Tokenization: The process of breaking text into smaller units (tokens) for AI processing.

5. Transformer Models: Neural network architectures, like GPT, designed for natural language processing tasks.

U

1. Unsupervised Learning: A machine learning approach where models learn patterns from unlabeled data.

2. User Experience (UX) AI: AI systems designed to improve user interactions with digital products.

3. Uncertainty Quantification: AI techniques used to measure and manage uncertainty in predictions.

4. Ubiquitous AI: AI systems integrated into everyday objects and environments.

5. Universal Basic Income (UBI): A socioeconomic concept often discussed in the context of AI-driven job displacement.

V

1. Virtual Assistant: AI-powered software agents that assist users with tasks, such as Siri or Alexa.

2. Virtual Reality (VR): Immersive technology often combined with AI for enhanced experiences.

3. Vision Transformers (ViTs): Transformer models adapted for computer vision tasks.

4. Voice Cloning: AI technology used to replicate a person's voice.

5. Validation Data: A dataset used to evaluate the performance of a trained AI model.

W

1. Weak AI: AI systems designed for specific tasks, lacking general intelligence.

2. Wearable AI: AI-powered devices worn on the body, such as smartwatches or fitness trackers.

3. Web Scraping: The use of AI to extract data from websites.

4. Weight Initialization: The process of setting initial parameters in neural networks.

5. Workflow Automation: The use of AI to streamline and automate business processes.

X

1. XAI (Explainable AI): AI systems designed to provide transparent and interpretable results.

2. XML (eXtensible Markup Language): A data format often used in AI for structuring information.

3. XGBoost: A popular machine learning algorithm for supervised learning tasks.

4. X-Ray Analysis: AI applications used to analyze medical X-ray images.

5. Xenobots: AI-designed biological robots created from living cells.

Y

1. YOLO (You Only Look Once): A real-time object detection algorithm used in computer vision.

2. Yield Optimization: AI techniques used to maximize efficiency in agriculture or manufacturing.

3. Yottabyte: A unit of data storage, relevant to the massive datasets used in AI.

4. Yottascale Computing: Future computing systems capable of processing yottabytes of data, enabling advanced AI.

5. Yottabit AI: Hypothetical AI systems capable of processing yottabit-scale data.

Z

1. Zero-Shot Learning: AI models capable of performing tasks they were not explicitly trained on.

2. Zettabyte: A unit of data storage, representing the vast amounts of data used in AI training.

3. Zigbee: A communication protocol used in IoT devices, often integrated with AI.

4. Z-Score Normalization: A statistical technique used in AI to standardize data.

5. Zombie AI: A colloquial term for AI systems that continue to operate without human oversight.

Timeline of AI Evolution

The evolution of Artificial Intelligence (AI) spans decades, marked by groundbreaking discoveries, technological advancements, and paradigm shifts. Below is a concise timeline highlighting key milestones in AI's development:

1950s: The Birth of AI

- 1950: Alan Turing publishes Computing Machinery and Intelligence, proposing the Turing Test as a measure of machine intelligence.
- 1956: The Dartmouth Conference is held, coining the term "Artificial Intelligence" and marking the official birth of AI as a field.

1960s: Early Optimism and Symbolic AI

- 1965: Joseph Weizenbaum develops ELIZA, the first chatbot, capable of simulating human conversation.
- 1969: Shakey the Robot, developed at Stanford, becomes the first general-purpose mobile robot capable of reasoning about its actions.

1970s: AI Winters and Challenges

- 1974-1980: The first AI Winter occurs, as funding and interest decline due to unmet expectations and technical limitations.
- 1979: Stanford Cart, an autonomous vehicle, successfully navigates a room, laying the groundwork for future robotics.

1980s: Expert Systems and Revival

- 1980s: Expert Systems gain popularity, using rule-based reasoning to solve specific problems in fields like medicine and engineering.

- 1986: Backpropagation is popularized, enabling more efficient training of neural networks.

1990s: Machine Learning and the Internet

- In 1997, IBM's Deep Blue triumphed over world chess champion Garry Kasparov, demonstrating AI's strategic potential.
- 1998: Yann LeCun develops LeNet-5, a pioneering convolutional neural network (CNN) for handwriting recognition.

2000s: Big Data and Deep Learning

- 2006: Geoffrey Hinton coins the term Deep Learning, sparking a resurgence in neural network research.

- 2009: ImageNet is launched, providing a massive dataset that fuels advancements in computer vision.

2010s: AI Goes Mainstream

- 2011: IBM's Watson wins Jeopardy!, demonstrating AI's ability to process natural language and complex queries.
- 2012: AlexNet wins the ImageNet competition, revolutionizing computer vision with deep learning.
- 2016: Google's AlphaGo defeats world champion Lee Sedol in the game of Go, a milestone in AI's strategic reasoning.
- 2018: OpenAI releases GPT, a transformer-based language model, transforming natural language processing (NLP).

2020s: Generative AI and AGI Aspirations

- In 2020, GPT-3 was launched, revealing remarkable advancements in text creation and comprehension.
- 2021: DALL·E and CLIP by OpenAI demonstrate AI's ability to generate images from text prompts.
- 2022: ChatGPT becomes a global phenomenon, bringing conversational AI to the mainstream.
- 2023: AI tools like MidJourney and Stable Diffusion revolutionize creative industries with generative art.

2025 and Beyond: The Future of AI

- 2025: AI is expected to achieve greater integration into daily life, with advancements in AGI, quantum AI, and AI ethics shaping its trajectory.
- 2030s and Beyond: The pursuit of Artificial General Intelligence (AGI)

continues, with AI potentially achieving human-like reasoning and adaptability.

AI Tools and Frameworks

The rapid advancement of Artificial Intelligence (AI) has been fueled by a wide array of tools and frameworks that simplify the development, training, and deployment of AI models. These tools cater to various aspects of AI, including machine learning, deep learning, natural language processing, and computer vision. Below is a brief overview of some of the most popular and impactful AI tools and frameworks:

1. Machine Learning Frameworks
- TensorFlow: Created by Google, TensorFlow is an open-source platform for machine learning and deep learning. It is widely used for building and deploying neural networks.

- PyTorch: Developed by Facebook's AI Research team, PyTorch is renowned for its adaptability and dynamic computation graph, making it popular among researchers.
- Scikit-learn: A Python library for traditional machine learning algorithms, ideal for tasks like classification, regression, and clustering.

2. Deep Learning Frameworks

- Keras: A high-level neural networks API, often used with TensorFlow, designed for fast experimentation and prototyping.
- MXNet: A scalable deep learning framework supported by Apache, known for its efficiency in training and deployment.

- Caffe: A deep learning framework optimized for speed, particularly in computer vision applications.

3. Natural Language Processing (NLP) Tools
- Hugging Face Transformers: A library offering pre-trained models like BERT, GPT, and T5 for NLP tasks such as text generation, translation, and sentiment analysis.
- spaCy: An industrial-strength NLP library for processing and analyzing text data.
- NLTK (Natural Language Toolkit): A Python library for working with human language data, often used in academic research.

4. Computer Vision Tools
- OpenCV: An open-source computer vision library with tools for image and

video processing, object detection, and facial recognition.

- YOLO (You Only Look Once): A real-time object detection system used for applications like autonomous vehicles and surveillance.

- Detectron2: Facebook AI Research's library for object detection and segmentation tasks.

5. AutoML and No-Code AI Platforms

- Google AutoML: A suite of tools that automates the process of training machine learning models, making AI accessible to non-experts.

- H2O.ai: An open-source platform for automated machine learning, offering tools for model building and deployment.

- DataRobot: A no-code AI platform that simplifies the end-to-end process of building and deploying machine learning models.

6. Reinforcement Learning Frameworks

- OpenAI Gym: A framework designed for creating and evaluating reinforcement learning algorithms.
- Stable-Baselines3: A collection of dependable reinforcement learning algorithm implementations using PyTorch.
- Ray RLlib: A scalable library for reinforcement learning, part of the Ray ecosystem.

7. AI Deployment and Monitoring Tools

- TensorFlow Serving: A flexible system for serving machine learning models in production environments.
- MLflow: An open-source tool designed to oversee the entire machine learning

lifecycle, covering experimentation, reproducibility, and deployment.

- Kubeflow: A Kubernetes-based platform for deploying, monitoring, and managing machine learning workflows.

8. Generative AI Tools

- DALL·E: OpenAI's model for generating images from text prompts.
- Stable Diffusion: An open-source generative AI model for creating high-quality images.
- GPT-4: OpenAI's advanced language model for text generation, summarization, and conversational AI.

9. Specialized AI Tools

- IBM Watson: A suite of AI tools for enterprise applications, including NLP, computer vision, and data analysis.

- Dialogflow: Google's platform for building conversational AI agents and chatbots.

- Rasa: An open-source platform for creating contextual AI assistants and chatbots.

10. Emerging Tools and Frameworks

- JAX: A high-speed library for numerical computing and machine learning, created by Google.

- Fast.ai: A library designed to make deep learning more accessible through simplified APIs and best practices.

- LangChain: A framework for building applications powered by large language models, enabling advanced NLP workflows.

AI Research Institutions and Labs

The rapid progress in Artificial Intelligence (AI) is driven by groundbreaking research conducted by leading institutions and labs worldwide. These organizations, often backed by academia, industry, and governments, are at the forefront of advancing AI technologies and applications. Below is a brief overview of some of the most influential AI research institutions and labs:

1. Academic Institutions

- MIT Computer Science and Artificial Intelligence Laboratory (CSAIL): One of the world's leading research centers, focusing on AI, robotics, and machine learning.

- Stanford AI Lab (SAIL): A pioneer in AI research, known for its contributions to natural language processing, computer vision, and robotics.
- Carnegie Mellon University (CMU): Home to the Robotics Institute and a leader in AI, machine learning, and autonomous systems.

2. Industry Research Labs
- OpenAI: A research organization focused on developing safe and beneficial artificial general intelligence (AGI), known for GPT and DALL·E.
- Google DeepMind: A leader in AI research, famous for breakthroughs like AlphaGo, AlphaFold, and reinforcement learning.
- Microsoft Research AI: Conducts cutting-edge research in AI, including NLP, computer vision, and ethical AI.

- Facebook AI Research (FAIR): Focuses on advancing AI in areas like computer vision, NLP, and reinforcement learning.
- IBM Research: Known for Watson, quantum computing, and AI applications in healthcare and enterprise.

3. Government and Non-Profit Organizations

- Allen Institute for AI (AI2): A non-profit research institute focused on AI for the common good, with projects in NLP, computer vision, and scientific AI.
- National Institute of Standards and Technology (NIST): Works on AI standards, ethics, and safety to ensure responsible AI development.
- Partnership on AI: A collaborative organization bringing together academia, industry, and NGOs to address AI's societal impacts.

4. International Research Hubs

- Vector Institute (Canada): A leading center for AI research, specializing in deep learning and its applications.

- Alan Turing Institute (UK): The UK's national institute for data science and AI, focusing on interdisciplinary research.

- AI Research Institutes (USA): Funded by the National Science Foundation (NSF), these institutes focus on areas like AI-driven innovation, optimization, and human-AI collaboration.

5. Emerging and Specialized Labs

- Baidu Research: Focuses on AI applications in areas like autonomous driving, NLP, and computer vision.

- Tencent AI Lab: Conducts research in machine learning, computer vision, and AI for gaming and healthcare.

- Samsung AI Center: Works on AI for consumer electronics, robotics, and healthcare.

AI Conferences and Events

AI conferences and events are pivotal in fostering collaboration, sharing groundbreaking research, and showcasing the latest advancements in artificial intelligence. These gatherings bring together researchers, industry leaders, policymakers, and enthusiasts to discuss trends, challenges, and opportunities in AI. Below is a brief overview of some of the most prominent AI conferences and events:

1. Leading Academic Conferences

- NeurIPS (Conference on Neural Information Processing Systems): One of the most prestigious AI conferences, focusing on deep learning, reinforcement learning, and neuroscience.

- ICML (International Conference on Machine Learning): A top-tier conference for cutting-edge research in machine learning algorithms and applications.

- CVPR (Conference on Computer Vision and Pattern Recognition): The premier event for advancements in computer vision, image processing, and pattern recognition.

- ACL (Annual Meeting of the Association for Computational Linguistics): A leading conference for natural language processing (NLP) and computational linguistics.

- AAAI (Association for the Advancement of Artificial Intelligence): Covers a broad range of AI topics, including ethics, robotics, and machine learning.

2. Industry-Focused Events

- Google I/O: Showcases Google's latest AI innovations, including updates on TensorFlow, Google AI, and DeepMind.

- Microsoft Build: Highlights Microsoft's AI tools and platforms, such as Azure AI and OpenAI integrations.

- NVIDIA GTC (GPU Technology Conference): Focuses on AI, deep learning, and GPU-accelerated computing.

- OpenAI DevDay: An event by OpenAI to announce new models, tools, and updates for developers.

3. Interdisciplinary and Applied AI Events

- AI for Good Global Summit (ITU): Explores how AI can address global challenges like healthcare, climate change, and education.

- AI Ethics and Society Conference: Focuses on the ethical, social, and policy implications of AI.
- Re-Work AI Events: A series of global summits on applied AI in industries like healthcare, finance, and robotics.

4. Regional and Emerging Conferences

- EMNLP (Conference on Empirical Methods in Natural Language Processing): A major NLP conference with a focus on empirical research.
- ICRA (International Conference on Robotics and Automation): A leading event for AI in robotics and autonomous systems.
- IJCAI (International Joint Conference on Artificial Intelligence): A global conference covering a wide range of AI topics.

5. Workshops and Competitions

- Kaggle Competitions: Hosted by Google, these competitions challenge data scientists to solve real-world problems using AI.

- AI Hackathons: Events where developers and researchers collaborate to build AI solutions in a short timeframe.

- AI Workshops at Major Conferences: Specialized sessions on topics like AI ethics, generative AI, and AI for social good.

Acknowledgments and References

This book is the culmination of extensive research and insights drawn from the works of leading experts and pioneers in the field of artificial intelligence (AI). We are deeply grateful to the researchers, authors, and organizations whose contributions have shaped the content of this book. Below, we acknowledge the key references and sources that have informed our understanding and analysis of the topics covered.

Key References

1. Russell, S., & Norvig, P. (2020). *Artificial Intelligence: A Modern Approach* (4th ed.). Pearson.

2. Sutton, R. S., & Barto, A. G. (2018). *Reinforcement Learning: An Introduction* (2nd ed.). MIT Press.

3. Goodfellow, I., Bengio, Y., & Courville, A. (2016). *Deep Learning*. MIT Press.

4. LeCun, Y., Bengio, Y., & Hinton, G. (2015). Deep Learning. *Nature*, 521(7553), 436-444.

5. Brown, T., et al. (2020). Language Models are Few-Shot Learners. *Advances in Neural Information Processing Systems (NeurIPS)*.

6. Devlin, J., Chang, M. W., Lee, K., & Toutanova, K. (2019). BERT: Pre-training of Deep Bidirectional Transformers for Language Understanding. NAACL-HLT.

7. Brynjolfsson, E., & McAfee, A. (2014). *The Second Machine Age: Work, Progress, and Prosperity in a Time of Brilliant Technologies*. W.W. Norton & Company.

8. Tegmark, M. (2017). *Life 3.0: Being Human in the Age of Artificial Intelligence*. Knopf.

9. Amodei, D., et al. (2016). Concrete Problems in AI Safety. *arXiv preprint arXiv:1606.06565*.

10. McMahan, B., et al. (2017). Communication-Efficient Learning of Deep Networks from Decentralized Data. *Proceedings of the 20th International Conference on Artificial Intelligence and Statistics (AISTATS)*.

11. Chen, T., Kornblith, S., Norouzi, M., & Hinton, G. (2020). A Simple Framework for Contrastive Learning of Visual Representations (SimCLR). *Proceedings of the 37th International Conference on Machine Learning (ICML)*.

12. Graves, A., Wayne, G., & Danihelka, I. (2014). Neural Turing Machines. *arXiv preprint arXiv:1410.5401*.

Section 1: Foundations of AI

1. Russell, S., & Norvig, P. (2020). Artificial Intelligence: A Modern Approach (4th ed.). Pearson.
2. Goodfellow, I., Bengio, Y., & Courville, A. (2016). Deep Learning. MIT Press.
3. LeCun, Y., Bengio, Y., & Hinton, G. (2015). Deep learning. Nature, 521(7553), 436-444.
4. Sutton, R. S., & Barto, A. G. (2018). Reinforcement Learning: An Introduction (2nd ed.). MIT Press.
5. Bostrom, N. (2014). Superintelligence: Paths, Dangers, Strategies. Oxford University Press.

Section 2: Emerging AI Technologies

1. Amodei, D., & Hernandez, D. (2018). AI and Compute. OpenAI Blog. Retrieved from

https://openai.com/blog/ai-and-compute

2. Shor, P. W. (1999). Polynomial-time algorithms for prime factorization and discrete logarithms on a quantum computer. SIAM Review, 41(2), 303-332.

3. Silver, D., et al. (2018). A general reinforcement learning algorithm that masters chess, shogi, and Go through self-play. Science, 362(6419), 1140-1144.

4. Gandomi, A., & Haider, M. (2015). Beyond the hype: Big data concepts, methods, and analytics. International Journal of Information Management, 35(2), 137-144.

5. Krizhevsky, A., Sutskever, I., & Hinton, G. E. (2012). ImageNet classification with deep convolutional neural networks. Advances in Neural Information Processing Systems, 25, 1097-1105.

Section 3: Ethical and Collaborative AI

1. Doshi-Velez, F., & Kim, B. (2017). Towards a rigorous science of interpretable machine learning. arXiv preprint arXiv:1702.08608.

2. McMahan, H. B., et al. (2017). Communication-efficient learning of deep networks from decentralized data. Proceedings of the 20th International Conference on Artificial Intelligence and Statistics, 54, 1273-1282.

3. Li, T., Sahu, A. K., Talwalkar, A., & Smith, V. (2020). Federated learning: Challenges, methods, and future directions. IEEE Signal Processing Magazine, 37(3), 50-60.

4. Arrieta, A. B., et al. (2020). Explainable Artificial Intelligence (XAI): Concepts, taxonomies, opportunities, and

challenges toward responsible AI.
Information Fusion, 58, 82-115.

5. Zhou, Z., Chen, X., Li, E., Zeng, L., Luo, K., & Zhang, J. (2019). Edge intelligence: Paving the last mile of artificial intelligence with edge computing. Proceedings of the IEEE, 107(8), 1738-1762.

Section 5: The Future of AI

1. Bostrom, N. (2014). Superintelligence: Paths, Dangers, Strategies. Oxford University Press.

2. Brynjolfsson, E., & McAfee, A. (2014). The Second Machine Age: Work, Progress, and Prosperity in a Time of Brilliant Technologies. W.W. Norton & Company.

3. Tegmark, M. (2017). Life 3.0: Being Human in the Age of Artificial Intelligence. Knopf.

4. Goertzel, B. (2014). Artificial General Intelligence: Concept, State of the Art, and Future Prospects. Springer.

5. Kaku, M. (2018). The Future of Humanity: Terraforming Mars, Interstellar Travel, Immortality, and Our Destiny Beyond Earth. Doubleday.

Section 6: Creative and Immersive AI

1. McCormack, J., Gifford, T., & Hutchings, P. (2019). Autonomy, authenticity, authorship, and intention in computer-generated art. International Conference on Computational Intelligence in Music, Sound, Art, and Design, 35-50.

2. Elgammal, A., Liu, B., Elhoseiny, M., & Mazzone, M. (2017). CAN: Creative adversarial networks, generating "art" by learning about styles and deviating from

style norms. Proceedings of the 8th International Conference on Computational Creativity, 96-103.

3. Bailenson, J. N. (2018). Experience on Demand: What Virtual Reality Is, How It Works, and What It Can Do. W.W. Norton & Company.

4. Park, S. M., & Kim, Y. G. (2022). A metaverse: Taxonomy, components, applications, and open challenges. IEEE Access, 10, 4209-4251.

5. Epstein, Z., et al. (2021). Art and the science of generative AI. Science, 372(6537), 458-459.

Dear Reader,

Thank you for joining me on this journey through **AI Trends in 2025**! I hope you're finding the book as engaging and meaningful as I intended it to be. Your thoughts and feedback mean a great deal to me.

If you've enjoyed the book so far, sharing your honest review on Amazon can help other readers discover it. Reviews are incredibly valuable, not only to authors like me but also to those searching for their next read.

Whether it's a quick note about what resonated with you or a detailed reflection, your feedback is always appreciated.

Book   link: https://www.amazon.com/dp/B0DRTK49ZN

Thank you for your time, support, and for being a part of this story.